PAIRED
PASSAGES

Grade 3

Credits
Content Editor: Lynette Pyne
Copy Editor: Karen Seberg

Visit *carsondellosa.com* for correlations to Common Core, state, national, and Canadian provincial standards.

Carson-Dellosa Publishing, LLC
PO Box 35665
Greensboro, NC 27425 USA
carsondellosa.com

ISBN 978-1-4838-3067-4
04-254171151

Table of Contents

Introduction

As students sharpen their reading comprehension skills, they become better readers. Improving these skills has never been more important as teachers struggle to meet the rigorous college- and career-ready expectations of today's educational standards.

This book offers pairings of high-interest fiction and nonfiction passages that will appeal to even the most reluctant readers. The passages have grade-level readability. Follow-up pages promote specific questioning based on evidence from the passages.

Throughout the book, students are encouraged to practice close reading, focusing on details to make inferences from each passage separately and then as a set. The text-dependent questions and activities that follow the passages encourage students to synthesize the information they have read, leading to deeper comprehension.

How to Use This Book

Three types of pairings divide this book: fiction with nonfiction, nonfiction with nonfiction, and fiction with fiction. The book is broken down further into 22 sets of paired passages that are combined with follow-up questions and activities. Each reading passage is labeled *Fiction* or *Nonfiction*.

The passages in this book may be used in any order but should be completed as four-page sets so that students read the passages in the correct pairs. The pairs of passages have been carefully chosen and each pair has topics or elements in common.

Two pages of questions and activities follow each pair of passages to support student comprehension. The questions and activities are based on evidence that students can find in the texts. No further research is required. Students will answer a set of questions that enable comprehension of each of the two passages. The questions range in format and include true/false, multiple choice, and short answer. The final questions or activities ask students to compare and contrast details or elements from the two passages.

Assessment Rubric

Use this rubric as a guide for assessing students' work. It can also be offered to students to help them check their work or as a tool to show your scoring.

4	_____ Independently reads and comprehends grade-level texts _____ Easily compares and contrasts authors' purposes _____ Uses higher-order thinking skills to link common themes or ideas _____ References both passages when comparing and contrasting _____ Skillfully summarizes reading based on textual evidence
3	_____ Needs little support for comprehension of grade-level texts _____ Notes some comparisons of authors' purposes _____ Infers broad common themes or ideas _____ Connects key ideas and general themes of both passages _____ Uses textual evidence to summarize reading with some support
2	_____ Needs some support for comprehension of grade-level texts _____ Understands overt similarities in authors' purposes _____ Links stated or obvious common themes or ideas _____ Compares and contrasts both passages with support _____ Summarizes reading based on textual evidence with difficulty
1	_____ Reads and comprehends grade-level text with assistance _____ Cannot compare or contrast authors' purposes _____ Has difficulty linking common themes or ideas _____ Cannot connect the information from both passages _____ Is unable to use textual evidence to summarize reading

Ant Farmers

It's easy to spot leaf-cutter ants. Just look for long lines of hundreds or even thousands of ants carrying small pieces of leaves over their heads. Ants often clear paths from their nests to their leafy food sources. This helps them march back and forth quickly and easily.

Leaf-cutter ants climb plants and trees and saw off bits of leaves with their powerful jaws. The leaf bits are often bigger than the ants are. These ants can carry up to 10 times their own weight. That's like a third grader carrying an adult zebra over his head!

Leaf-cutter ants trek back in long lines to their underground nest. The nest may have over 1,000 rooms connected by tunnels. Millions of ants live together there. The ants are different sizes, and each size has a different job. They are workers, soldiers, queens, or guards. No single ant is in charge. Each ant has its job and does it.

Leaf-cutter ants are the farmers of the insect world. Deep down in this huge nest are fungus "gardens." The ants bring their leaf clippings here. New leaves are chewed by worker ants, mixed with saliva, and fertilized. The newest leaf bits are placed on top of the garden. Underneath, older bits grow into nutritious food.

The smallest ants have the job of "farming" the fungus gardens. Sometimes, a part of the garden may start to go bad. The ant farmers squirt acid from their bodies on that section of the garden to keep poisons from growing there.

The fungus gardens are important. They provide extra food for the entire colony. All of the ants work together to ensure that the colony has plenty of food.

The Ants and the Grasshopper
by Aesop (adapted)

One bright day in late autumn, a family of ants was bustling about in the cool sunshine, drying out the grain they had stored up during the summer. A hungry grasshopper, his fiddle under his arm, came up and humbly begged them for a bite to eat.

"What!" the ants cried in surprise. "Haven't you stored anything away for the winter? What in the world were you doing all last summer?"

"I didn't have time to store up any food," the grasshopper whined. "I was so busy making music that before I knew it, the summer was gone."

The ants shrugged their shoulders in disgust.

"Making music, were you?" they cried. "Very well. Now, dance!" And they turned their backs on the grasshopper and went on with their work.

Name _____

Answer the questions.

I. What was the author's purpose in writing "The Ants and the Grasshopper"?

   A. to teach readers about insects

   B. to describe the problems grasshoppers have in winter

   C. to teach a lesson

   D. to show how ants prepare for winter

2. According to "The Ants and the Grasshopper," why did the ants have plenty to eat in late autumn?

   A. The ants stored up grain during the summer months.

   B. Food was plentiful for the ants all year long.

   C. The ants never worried about meals.

   D. The grasshopper brought food for the ants.

3. What is the main idea of "Ant Farmers"?

   A. Ants can lift more than 10 times their own weight.

   B. Ants work together to feed their colony.

   C. Leaf-cutter ants live in large nests.

   D. Ants are amazing creatures.

4. According to "Ant Farmers," how do ants work together to feed themselves?

   A. Large leaf-cutter ants climb plants and trees to find leaves.

   B. Small ants take care of an underground garden.

   C. Ant farmers squirt acid on the bad parts of the garden.

   D. all of the above

5. What is the moral, or lesson, of "The Ants and the Grasshopper"?

   A. Work hard in the summertime.

   B. Don't make music or you will starve.

   C. There is a time for work and a time for play.

   D. Ants and grasshoppers do not get along.

6. Gathering and storing food is very important to many species of animals. Complete the chart with details about the physical and community features that help ants feed themselves. Read the passages again if you need help.

	The Ants and the Grasshopper	**Ant Farmers**
Physical Features		
Community Features		

7. Based on the chart in question 6, write a summary comparing the two passages about ants.

_____

_____

_____

_____

_____

_____

_____

The Oregon Trail

The Oregon Trail was a path pioneers followed to get to the West. Pioneers wanted to start farms in new places. Many people traveled along the trail in large covered wagons.

Pioneers had to leave most of their things behind. Food, tools, and clothing were packed into the wagons. People brought bacon, beans, coffee, and flour to eat. Many packed tents to sleep in. They brought tools like shovels and axes for building things. Oxen were used to pull the wagons over the trail. People would often walk beside their wagons as they moved along.

The trail began in Missouri and stretched all of the way to Oregon. It was many miles long and went through five different states. The trail was rough. Pioneers had to cross the Rocky Mountains. That was the most dangerous part of the journey. It took most pioneers about five months to make the trip.

Many people used the trail until a railroad was built. The railroad was a faster and safer way to travel to the West. Today, much of the trail has been built over, but some of it remains. Visitors can still see the tracks made by the wagon wheels.

Tales from the Oregon Trail

July 20, 1848

We have been traveling for many weeks now. It seems like it was so long ago that we left our farm. My little brother is still excited about the trip, but I want to go home. I miss my friends. I miss my old life on the farm.

My family has spent most of our money buying food and tools for the trip. Our wagon is so full. I fear it will tip over each time the oxen turn. Other families have much more food than we have. We plan to hunt along the way. Each day we see herds of elk and buffalo. It will be a nice change to eat something other than beans and bacon.

Yesterday, we found an abandoned wagon. I wondered what happened to the people who were traveling in it, but we needed the extra supplies. We found two wagon wheels and some used cooking pots.

I have begun to make friends with other families on the trail. We explore together and help gather food. Ma needs me to look after my little brother and help cook meals for us. Traveling on the trail is so much more work than living on the farm. I long for the day when we finally have a home.

by Abigail Edwards, age 15

Name _____

Answer the questions.

1. What was the author's purpose in writing "The Oregon Trail"?

   A. to teach readers about pioneers

   B. to teach readers about covered wagons

   C. to teach a lesson

   D. to show how pioneers caught food

2. According to "The Oregon Trail," why did pioneers want to travel to the West?

   A. to begin life in a new place

   B. to hunt buffalo and elk

   C. to see different places

   D. to go on vacation

3. What is the main idea of "Tales from the Oregon Trail"?

   _____

   _____

   _____

4. Write **true** or **false**.

   _____ Pioneers were people who traveled to the West.

5. According to "Tales from the Oregon Trail," what was one chore the author had?

   A. feeding the animals

   B. looking after a younger brother

   C. mending clothing

   D. getting water from rivers and streams

Name _____

6. The Oregon Trail was a long and difficult journey. Complete the chart with details about pioneers and people today. Read the passages again if you need help.

	Pioneer Times	**Today**
Travel		
Getting Food		
Chores		

7. Why was life for pioneers so difficult? Use the information in the chart above to help you write your answer.

_____

_____

_____

_____

_____

_____

_____

Trail of Tears

The Cherokee people had lived on their land for a long time. They farmed and hunted deer, bear, and elk for food. When pioneers and settlers began to arrive, they wanted the land that the Cherokee people used. The American government made a law saying that the Cherokee had to leave. They were told to move to a place now known as Oklahoma.

But, the Cherokee did not want to leave. They wanted to live like they always had. The US army was ordered to capture the people and force them to move. Their journey is known as the Trail of Tears.

The Trail of Tears is a group of trails and rivers that the Cherokee walked or boated on to get to Oklahoma. Most of the people were forced to walk the entire way. They walked through the cold, rain, snow, and heat. There was not enough water or food. Most did not have the proper clothing or shoes for such a long trip.

The Cherokee people were treated harshly by the soldiers who led them on the trail. Many became very ill and suffered badly. Families were not allowed to stop to help the sick. They were forced to leave them behind. More than 4,000 people died on the long journey. The Trail of Tears marks a very sad time in American history.

A Sad Day

One morning last summer, I awoke to find soldiers at my family's home. They told us we needed to leave right away. They were taking us to our new land in Oklahoma. Our family has lived on this land for a very long time. My father begged for them to let us stay. But, we were told to leave quickly. We grabbed whatever food and small things we could carry and fled.

It is now winter, and we have been walking for many months. It is very cold, and my shoes are wearing out. We walk through the pouring rain and falling snow. Sometimes, we come to a river or stream where we can get water. When we are given food, I try to share it with the younger children or elders. The trip has been hardest for them. At night, we sleep on the ground until the sun rises. Then, we start our journey again. It seems like it will never end.

The cold and wet weather has made so many people sick. There are no doctors to take care of us. We do what we can to help each other, but there is no rest on this journey. Most will suffer terribly from being hungry, cold, or sick.

I miss my home and our land. I am afraid that more of my family will suffer before we reach Oklahoma. My only hope is that the worst times are finally behind us.

Name _____

Answer the questions.

I. According to "Trail of Tears," why did the Cherokee people have to leave their lands?

_____

_____

_____

2. Why did the author write "Trail of Tears"?

_____

_____

_____

3. Write **true** or **false**.

_____ The Cherokee were treated kindly on the Trail of Tears.

4. According to "A Sad Day," who took the Cherokee away from their homes?

   A. soldiers

   B. police officers

   C. the president

   D. bandits

5. How did the author of "A Sad Day" feel?

   A. joyful

   B. excited

   C. homesick

   D. angry

6. The Cherokee were forced to move to what place?

   A. Georgia

   B. North Carolina

   C. Tennessee

   D. Oklahoma

7. Complete the organizer to show what happened to the Cherokee, the settlers, and the land.

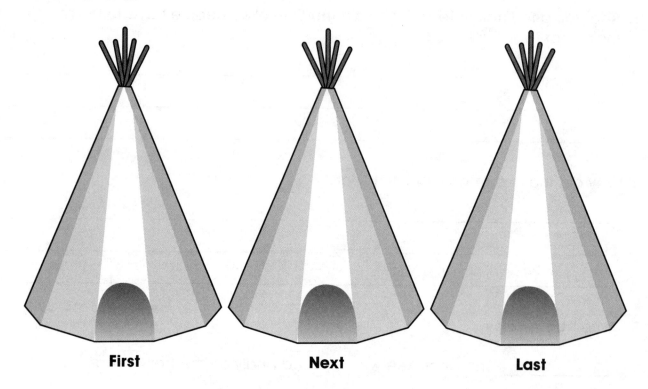

First   **Next**   **Last**

8. How do you think the Cherokee felt when they were forced to leave their land and homes? Use evidence from the text to support your answer.

_____

_____

_____

_____

_____

_____

_____

_____

_____

_____

_____

The San Francisco Earthquake

In 1906, a large earthquake shook the city of San Francisco. The city had experienced earthquakes before. But, this one was different. Even though it lasted less than one minute, it caused a great deal of damage. The shaking was felt for hundreds of miles.

Earthquakes happen when plates under Earth's surface move. These plates can move apart or bump into each other. This makes the ground above shake. Most earthquakes only cause a little shaking for a short time. But sometimes, the shaking is strong. It can knock down buildings. It can tip over large trees.

The large earthquake in San Francisco caused many fires. Much of the damage to the city was caused by these fires after the earthquake was over. The fires burned down people's homes and businesses. Without water to fight them, fires continued to burn for many days. People were afraid to stay inside buildings, so they built tents in the streets. They cooked food and lived outside in the tents for many weeks.

Today, scientists called seismologists study earthquakes. They use tools to measure how Earth's surface moves. They use this information to figure out where the next earthquakes may happen.

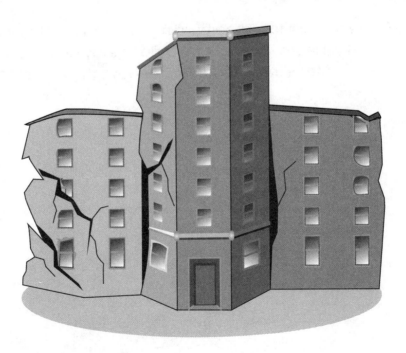

The Day the City Shook

Early one morning, Lita was awakened by the floor moving beneath her. The bed swayed. The walls were shaking. She held onto her bed to keep from falling and covered her head with her pillow. When the shaking eased up, Lita ran to the room where her father and mother slept. They were frightened too. Her parents said they needed to leave the house quickly and find a safer place.

In the kitchen, broken glass and dishes covered the floor. The windows had shattered. Furniture had toppled over. When Lita looked outside, she saw lots of confused and scared people lining the street, many still in their nightclothes. Lita's parents did not know where to go, but they knew they had to stay together.

Every few minutes, the house would gently shake again. Lita's father decided it would be safer to go outside than stay indoors. Her mother gathered some old sacks. She also grabbed some food from the pantry and refrigerator. They quickly dressed in several layers of clothing and headed outside. The three ran to an empty lot nearby with no trees or buildings.

After things calmed down, Lita and her mother stitched the sacks together. Then, Lita and her father used them to make a tent. They dug a hole in the ground and lined it with old bricks to make a stove. The family did not know if their home was still standing. None of them knew how long they might have to live outside.

Thick smoke filled the air from the large buildings burning blocks away. Gray ash floated down from the sky. Nearby homes and buildings lay crumbled and twisted. But, Lita and her family were grateful to be together. For now, they felt safe again.

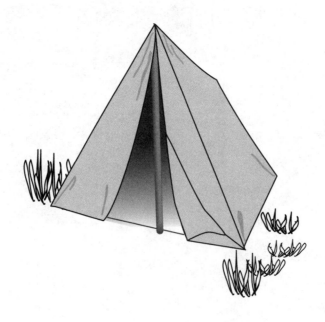

Name _____

Answer the questions.

1. What was the author's main purpose in writing "The San Francisco Earthquake"?

    A. to teach readers about fires

    B. to encourage readers to visit the city

    C. to inform readers about an important event

    D. to explain how scientists study earthquakes

2. In "The San Francisco Earthquake," what did not happen on that day?

    A. A large earthquake struck the city.

    B. Many fires started.

    C. A rainstorm caused a flood.

    D. Buildings and homes were destroyed.

3. How did the author of "The Day the City Shook" feel throughout the passage?

    _____

    _____

    _____

4. According to "The Day the City Shook," why did people go outside?

    A. to get some fresh air

    B. to find a safer place

    C. to talk to their neighbors

    D. to wait for help

5. According to "The San Francisco Earthquake," what does a seismologist study?

    _____

    _____

Name _____

6. Complete the chart to compare the sequence of events in each passage.

	First	**Next**	**Last**
The San Francisco Earthquake			
The Day the City Shook			

7. Based on what you read, write about the effects of an earthquake.

_____

_____

_____

_____

_____

_____

_____

_____

_____

Colors in the Sky

Look up in the sky on a rainy day, and you may see a beautiful rainbow. A rainbow is an arc of color in the sky. Look for a rainbow when it is rainy in one part of the sky and sunny in another part. Rainbows can also be seen in mist, fog, and dew. Red, orange, yellow, green, blue, indigo, and violet are the colors in a rainbow. Sir Isaac Newton was the scientist who figured out how rainbows are formed.

The rainbow got its name from its shape. The **arc**, or curve, of a rainbow looks like a bow for shooting arrows. Every tiny drop of rain creates its own rainbow. Millions of raindrops combine to make a rainbow in the sky.

You can never see the end of a rainbow. When you move, the rainbow also seems to move. The best place to see a rainbow is near a waterfall.

Rainbows are interesting. Did you know that no two people see exactly the same rainbow? It looks different to each person. And, there is no way to touch a rainbow.

You can make your own rainbow on a sunny day with a water hose. Stand with your back to the sun. Spray the water in front of you. Watch closely. Soon a rainbow will appear.

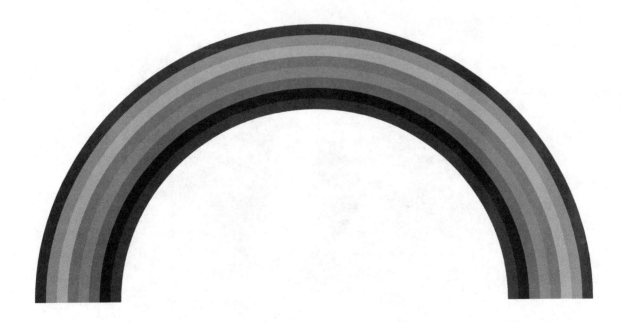

Painting a Rainbow
A Legend of the Ojibwe

Long ago, a young man lived in a house beside a waterfall. While walking one day, he noticed that all of the flowers around him were white. They did not have any colors at all. They were not pleasant to look at. He hurried back home and gathered up his paints. He had red, orange, yellow, green, blue, indigo, and violet paint. He put each color in its own pot.

He sat beside the waterfall and painted each flower with a beautiful color. Two birds were flying above him as he worked. Each time they passed by, they flew closer to the paint pots. Eventually a bird flew so close, his wing dipped into the red paint. As he flew through the waterfall mist, he left a red streak in the sky.

The second bird soon dipped her wing into the orange paint. As she flew through the mist, she left an orange streak in the sky. The birds continued dipping their wings into the paint and flying through the mist until all of the colors were above the waterfall.

When the young man looked up, he saw the streaks of color above. "You made a rainbow!" he said to the birds. He was so pleased at the sight, he left the rainbow above the waterfall for always.

Name _____

Answer the questions.

    I. According to "Colors in the Sky," what two things are needed to create a rainbow?

    _____

    _____

    2. As used in "Colors in the Sky," what does the word **arc** mean?

        A. circle

        B. curve

        C. star

        D. oval

    3. In "Painting a Rainbow," what colors were used to paint the flowers?

    _____   _____   _____

    _____   _____   _____

    _____

    4. In "Painting a Rainbow," what did the birds use to paint the sky?

        A. their beaks

        B. their wings

        C. their tails

        D. their feet

    5. In "Painting a Rainbow," how did the young man feel when he saw the rainbow?

        A. pleased

        B. annoyed

        C. bored

        D. tired

6. Complete the chart to show how a rainbow was made and what was used to create it in each passage.

	Colors in the Sky	Painting a Rainbow
How was a rainbow made?		
What was used to create it?		

7. Which passage gives you facts about rainbows? Explain your answer.

_____

_____

_____

_____

_____

_____

_____

_____

_____

Friends in the Sea

Dolphins are amazing animals. They live in families called pods. They take care of their babies and protect each other. Many stories are told about dolphins being very friendly toward humans. Old sea stories tell about dolphins saving people from drowning or from sharks. There are even stories of dolphins leading boats through rough waters.

When their babies are born, dolphins help them to the surface. They do this by swimming under them. Then, they use their snouts to push them up. Humans have told stories of dolphins helping them in the same way when they could not swim. Like humans, dolphins are mammals and breathe air with their lungs. They are also very smart.

In 2004, a group of divers were stranded in the Red Sea. They had gotten lost and could not find their boat. The divers were in the ocean for many hours waiting to be rescued. When a rescue boat finally arrived, the rescuers said dolphins were leaping in the direction of the lost divers. The divers believe dolphins helped lead the boat to find them.

Another story was told by a group of swimmers in New Zealand. A shark was swimming toward them. A family of dolphins made a circle around the swimmers. The dolphins herded the people together and slapped the water with their tails until the shark left.

Because humans cannot talk to dolphins, we do not know why they help people. It may be that they want to help fellow mammals. Maybe dolphins are more like us than we think!

Arion
A Greek Myth

Long ago, there lived a boy named Arion. He loved to sing and play his **lyre**, or harp. He was known throughout the town for his beautiful voice.

One day, news reached his town about a singing contest in another city. A large bag of gold and jewels would be given to the winner. Arion did not care much about the prize or winning the contest. He just loved singing more than anything. He also loved visiting new places. He decided he would sing in the contest.

The king and judges were surprised to hear Arion sing. They loved his wonderful voice. They awarded him the prize. They asked Arion to stay in their city. But, he had promised his family he would return. Soon, he boarded a ship for home.

While on the ship, Arion was surrounded by the sailors. They wanted Arion's prize. Arion said he would give them the prize if they did not hurt him. The sailors did not want Arion to tell others what they did. So, they decided to throw Arion into the ocean. Arion's only wish was to sing one last song.

While he was singing, a group of dolphins began swimming around the ship. When Arion was thrown into the water, a wise dolphin caught him on his back. The dolphins carried Arion safely back to land. Arion quickly told his story to the king. The angry king punished the sailors for their **wicked** deed.

Name _____

Answer the questions.

I. In "Arion," what kind of contest did the character enter?

_____

_____

2. As used in "Arion," what does the word **lyre** mean?

A. a guitar   **B.** a piano

C. a harp   **D.** a drum

3. What was the author's purpose for writing "Arion"?

_____

_____

_____

4. What was the author's purpose in writing "Friends in the Sea"?

_____

_____

_____

5. According to "Friends in the Sea," what is a family of dolphins called?

A. a pod   **B.** a group

C. a litter   **D.** a herd

6. As used in "Arion," what does the word **wicked** mean?

A. funny   **B.** evil

C. clever   **D.** pleasant

Name _____

7. Describe the main idea, characters, problems, and solution in each passage. Read the passages again if you need help. Use a separate sheet of paper if needed.

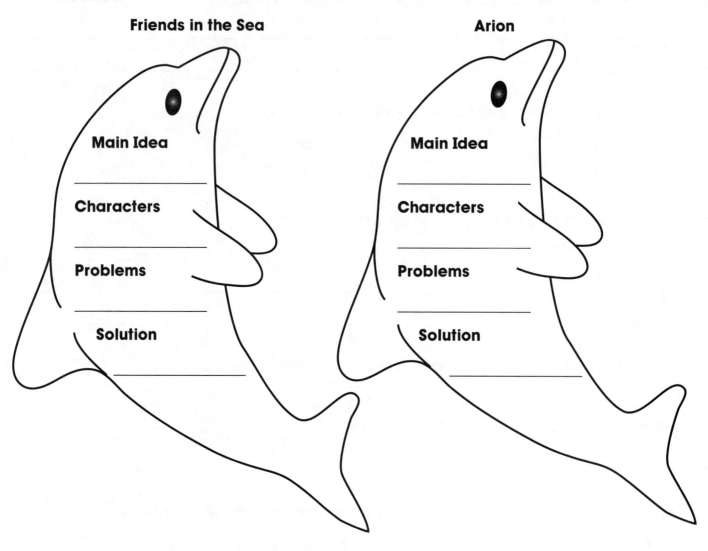

Friends in the Sea

Main Idea

_____

Characters

_____

Problems

_____

Solution

_____

Arion

Main Idea

_____

Characters

_____

Problems

_____

Solution

_____

8. Write about how dolphins have helped people. How does this make them different from other sea animals?

_____

_____

_____

_____

_____

_____

Tide Pools

Tide pools are like tiny **aquariums**. Many ocean animals and plants can be found in these unique places. Tide pools are small pools of seawater left behind when the tide goes out. They can be found along sandy beaches or rocky shorelines. They are full of sea life.

What lives in a tide pool? Sea stars, sea urchins, and sand dollars are often discovered here. Barnacles and mussels can be found attached to rocks in tide pools. Small crabs and shrimp also make their homes in tide pools. Plants such as seaweed, or marine algae, provide hiding places for creatures in the tide pool.

The best time to see the animals in a tide pool is when the tide goes out. Because waves often crash over them, the animals cling to rocks or hide underneath them. They need to hang on tight, or they will be swept away.

Sea creatures in tide pools also have to protect themselves from the sun. Crabs and shrimp can dig into the sand or crawl under seaweed or rocks. Mussels and other creatures with shells hide inside to stay safe. This helps keep them from being eaten by seagulls and other predators looking for an easy meal.

If you look closely you can see all kinds of sea life in a tide pool. When exploring, remember that a tide pool is home for many animals. If you lift up a rock or peek under a plant, be sure to put it back. Always be gentle and look carefully where you are stepping. Tide pools are amazing habitats!

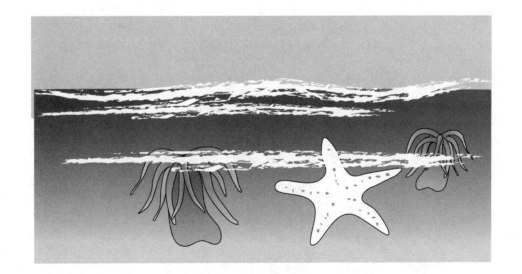

A Home on the Beach

Dear Maria,

I'm having the best time at the beach this week! I've been swimming in the ocean and building sandcastles on the beach. Yesterday, I went exploring with my mom and brother. We walked down the beach to some large rocks. After the tide went out, we saw puddles of water around rocks. My mom said they were tide pools. We put on sneakers and climbed slowly and carefully on the rocks. The closer you look, the more sea animals you find!

I gently lifted a rock and found a sea star. I asked my mom if I could pick it up, but she said, "Let it stay safely in its home." Animals like sea stars and sea urchins have to hide from the sun and other animals that will try to eat them. They are good at finding hiding places!

I looked around the rocks and found mussels with barnacles attached to them. When the waves came in, the mussels would stay put. Holding onto the rocks kept them from being washed away. My brother moved a piece of seaweed and found an oyster beneath it. It was using its shell as a safe hiding place.

We had to be careful to not step on any creatures or plants in the tide pool. When it was time to leave, I begged my mom to take the sea star home. She reminded me that tide pool creatures do not make good pets. They need to be in their natural habitats, or homes, to survive. I cannot wait to tell you more when I see you again!

Your friend,

Samantha

Name _____

Answer the questions.

I. According to "Tide Pools," how does a tide pool form?

_____

_____

_____

2. As used in "Tide Pools," what does the word **aquarium** mean?

    A. a place to view sea creatures   **B.** a place to view pets

    C. a place to view boats   **D.** a place to view sand and rocks

3. What was the author's purpose in writing "Tide Pools"?

_____

_____

_____

4. What was the author's purpose in writing "A Home on the Beach"?

_____

_____

_____

5. According to "A Home on the Beach," what should people *not* do when exploring tide pools?

    A. put back rocks that they move

    B. be careful where they walk

    C. leave the sea animals in the tide pool

    D. take the sea animals home as pets

6. Name three animals or plants that live in a tide pool.

_____

_____

Name _____

7. Complete the chart to compare how plants and animals adapt to tide pools.

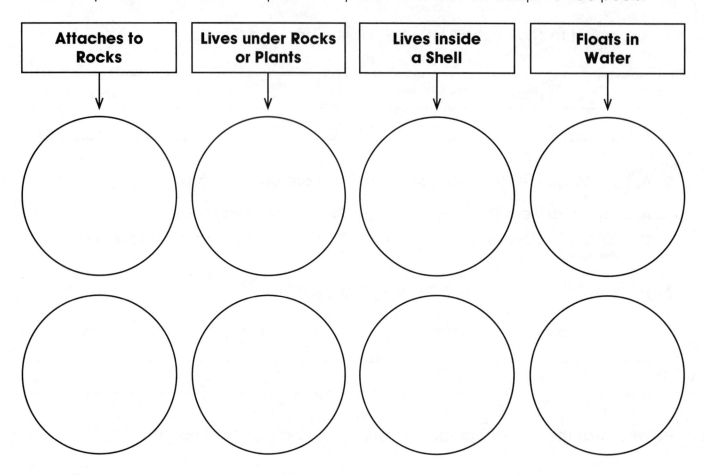

Attaches to Rocks	Lives under Rocks or Plants	Lives inside a Shell	Floats in Water

8. Write several important things to remember when exploring a tide pool.

_____

_____

_____

_____

_____

_____

_____

_____

_____

A Cowboy's Life

When people think of the Wild West, cowboys almost always come to mind. These Wild West cowboys were really cattle herders. They spent most of their lives working outside. They were away from home for long periods of time. A cowboy's life was very hard.

A cowboy's most important job was to care for large herds of cattle. The land out west was **arid**, or dry. That meant the cattle had to roam for miles to find food and water. Cowboys would ride along on horseback with the herds of cattle. Sometimes, they would drive the cattle back to a ranch for the night.

Cowboys wore clothes that would protect them from the hot daytime sun. The clothes also had to keep them warm in the cooler evenings. Clothing had to be tough since it was worn for weeks at a time. Cowboys wore denim jeans with leather covers, or chaps, to protect their legs. Wide-brimmed hats would protect them from the sun. A hat could even be used as a drinking bowl for a cowboy and his horse. A neckerchief was worn around the neck. It could be pulled up over a cowboy's mouth and nose to keep out dust.

Cowboys also kept their herds safe from animals such as cougars and wolves. Cattle rustlers might try to steal cattle, so cowboys always had to watch over them carefully. A successful cowboy returned to the ranch with a healthy cattle herd.

Cowboys Wanted

Do you like the outdoors? Do you like working with animals? Do you like to travel? Then, a cowboy's life may be for you!

The Happy Trails Ranch is looking for cowboys to help guide cattle across Texas to our ranch. Cowboys will need to stay with the herd as they roam the plains looking for food and water in the morning. Then, they must round up the herd and drive them along the trail. Each cowboy will be given a horse to ride during the trip.

There are several different jobs cowboys will have while on the trail. Two cowboys are needed to ride in front of the herd with the lead steers, or cattle, in front. They will guide the cattle in the right direction on the trail. Swing riders are needed to ride on each side of the herd. They will make sure no cattle wander away or get hurt. Several trail riders are needed to ride behind the herd. They will need to make sure the smaller and weaker cattle keep up with the herd.

We also need a chuck-wagon cook. This person will drive a covered wagon filled with food and cooking supplies. The cook will ride several miles ahead of the herd and look for a good place to stop and eat. A place with water is best so that the herd can drink and rest. The cook will make food for the cowboys over a campfire. Beans, coffee, and biscuits are favorite items to prepare.

What an adventure! If you are interested, see the trail boss, or the cowboy in charge.

Name _____

Answer the questions.

1. According to "A Cowboy's Life," what was a cowboy's most important job?

_____

_____

_____

2. As used in "A Cowboy's Life," what does the word **arid** mean?

   A. wet

   B. grassy

   C. dry

   D. green

3. What was the author's purpose for writing "A Cowboy's Life"?

_____

_____

_____

4. Write **true** or **false**.

   _____ A cowboy kept cattle in the herd together and safe.

5. According to "Cowboys Wanted," who is the trail boss?

   A. the cattle

   B. the rancher

   C. the cook

   D. the cowboy in charge

6. Name two jobs for a cowboy.

_____

_____

7. Complete the chart to tell about a cowboy's work, clothing, and food.

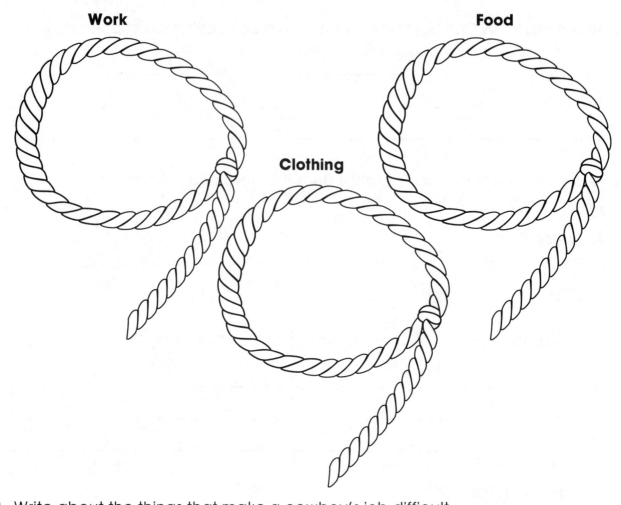

Work

Food

Clothing

8. Write about the things that make a cowboy's job difficult.

_____

_____

_____

_____

_____

_____

_____

_____

_____

A Bug-Eating Plant

Most insects eat plants. They will munch on the leaves. They will eat the fruits and flowers that grow on a plant. But, some special plants eat bugs instead! One of these bug-eating plants is called the Venus flytrap.

A Venus flytrap has two large leaves that trap flies and other insects. The leaves produce a sweet nectar. The insect is attracted to the nectar and lands on one of the leaves. There are small hairs on the leaves. When an insect touches them, the leaves snap shut. The insect is stuck inside and cannot get out.

The Venus flytrap has special enzymes inside its trap that digest the insects it catches. Your stomach has enzymes that help digest the food you eat too. It takes about 10 days for the plant to digest an insect. Then, the trap will open again to catch another meal.

Trapping bugs helps the Venus flytrap survive in its environment. The soil where the plant is usually found does not have enough nutrients for it to thrive and grow. Just as you eat healthy foods each day to help you grow, catching and eating insects helps the Venus flytrap grow.

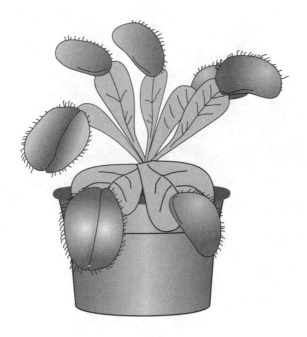

The Hunting Spider

Most spiders build webs to catch food. They hide and wait for insects to get caught in their webs. The trap-door spider catches its food in a unique way. It hunts for its prey. It builds a trap to catch its food.

The trap-door spider digs a hole or tunnel to live inside. Next, it spins a silk door for the hole's entrance. It might camouflage the door with soil or tiny plants. The door is very hard to see when it is shut. The spider leaves the door open a crack to peek through. The trap-door spider has good eyesight. It is able to see insects from far away. It will wait patiently for an insect to wander by. When an insect crawls too close, the spider jumps out and grabs it.

A trap-door spider has sharp fangs with poison in them. The poison helps the spider subdue insects much larger than itself. It can catch grasshoppers, crickets, and beetles. The poison keeps the insects from escaping once they are caught.

Trap-door spiders are clever at hiding behind the silk doors that cover their traps. Using a different way of hunting is their way to **adapt** and survive.

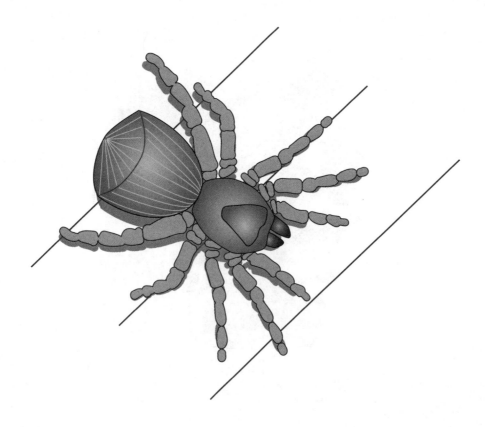

Name _____

Answer the questions.

1. What was the author's purpose in writing "A Bug-Eating Plant"?

    A. to teach readers about insects

    B. to teach readers about a special kind of plant

    C. to teach readers how to grow plants

    D. to show how farmers grow plants

2. According to "A Bug-Eating Plant," how does the plant catch its food?

    _____

    _____

    _____

3. What is the main idea of "The Hunting Spider"?

    A. It tells the reader the spider bites.

    B. It tells the reader what the spider looks like.

    C. It tells the reader how the spider builds its home.

    D. It tells the reader how the spider catches its food.

4. As used in "The Hunting Spider," what does the word **adapt** mean?

    A. to survive

    B. to adjust

    C. to live

    D. to go somewhere else

5. Number the steps to show how the spider builds its trap in "The Hunting Spider."

    _____ The spider spins a door out of silk.

    _____ The spider hides behind the door to wait for an insect.

    _____ The spider digs a hole or tunnel.

Name _____

6. Some living things use unique ways to catch prey. Complete the chart to tell how the Venus flytrap and trap-door spider catch food. Read the passages again if you need help.

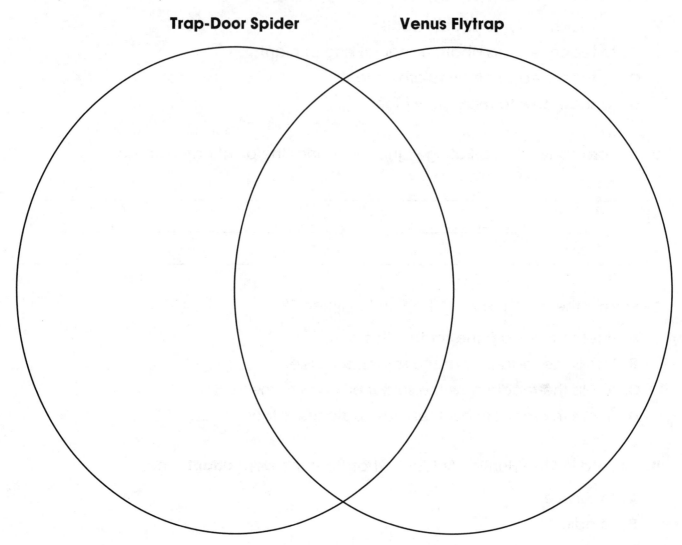

Trap-Door Spider   **Venus Flytrap**

7. Write about how the Venus flytrap and trap-door spider have adapted to their environments.

_____

_____

_____

_____

_____

First to Fly

Every day, airplanes fly to places all over the world. People can travel just about anywhere in an airplane. But, how did the airplane come to be in the first place?

Orville and Wilbur Wright invented the first airplane. They were the first to fly in a heavier-than-air machine. It took many years for them to make a machine that could stay in the air and run on its own power. They wanted to find a way for people to travel a long way in a short time.

The brothers enjoyed inventing things. They became interested in flying as boys after they got a toy helicopter as a gift. Orville and Wilbur often built their own helicopters, gliders, and kites. They were always testing their machines. They built many airplanes that crashed. Some didn't fly at all. But, the Wright Brothers **persevered** and kept trying.

Oliver and Wilbur wanted a good location to test their newest airplane. They chose Kitty Hawk, North Carolina. It was a place with lots of wind. There was a large sand dune to catch the plane if it crashed. Orville piloted the plane as it rose into the air. It stayed in the air for 12 seconds and went 120 feet (36.6 m). Orville and Wilbur were finally successful. The Wright Brothers had invented the airplane!

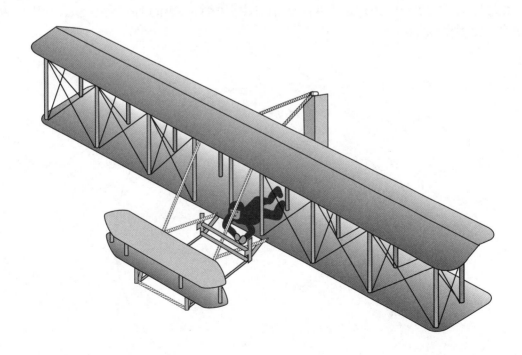

Walking on the Moon

In 1969, Neil Armstrong did something amazing. He became the first person to walk on the moon. He is famous for saying, "That's one small step for (a) man, one giant leap for mankind." He wanted people to know that traveling to the moon was no longer just a dream.

There is no oxygen on the moon. People need oxygen to breathe. Armstrong wore a special space suit so that he could breathe while on the moon. There is also less gravity on the moon than on Earth. That means astronauts could jump higher on the moon.

Neil Armstrong and his fellow astronaut Buzz Aldrin were on the moon for about two and one-half hours. They collected soil and rocks to take back to Earth. They also left an American flag on the moon. It is a reminder of the great feat they **accomplished** that day.

The *Apollo 11* moon-landing trip was very exciting to people back home on Earth. A camera was placed on the lunar module landing spacecraft. It took pictures of the astronauts while they were on the moon. Half a billion people watched as Armstrong stepped onto the moon's surface.

Other astronauts have traveled to the moon since Neil Armstrong's visit. They even brought a vehicle called the *Lunar Rover* to drive around in on the moon. This helped astronauts explore much more of the moon. Neil Armstrong helped pave the way for others to visit the moon.

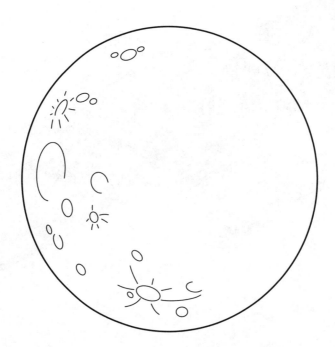

Name _____

Answer the questions.

1. According to "First to Fly," what did the Wright Brothers invent and why was their invention important?

   _____

   _____

   _____

2. As used in "First to Fly," what does the word **persevered** mean?

   A. kept trying

   B. had help from others

   C. went on a trip

   D. gave up

3. In "Walking on the Moon," what was extra special about Neil Armstrong's accomplishment?

   _____

   _____

   _____

4. As used in "Walking on the Moon," what does the word **accomplished** mean?

   A. stopped trying

   B. hid from something

   C. did successfully

   D. taught something

5. Write **true** or **false**.

   _____ Neil Armstrong left an American flag on the moon.

Name _____

6. Both Neil Armstrong and the Wright Brothers were the first to do something no one else had done. Complete the chart to compare what they each did.

	Neil Armstrong	**Wright Brothers**
Traveling Machine		
First To		

7. Write about how the accomplishments of Neil Armstrong and the Wright Brothers have made a difference in how people have traveled since then.

_____

_____

_____

_____

_____

_____

_____

_____

An Armored Animal

Have you seen an interesting animal that has its own built-in suit of armor? It's the only mammal with this kind of covering. Some people say it looks like a dinosaur. This unique animal is the armadillo.

The word *armadillo* means "little armored thing" in Spanish. The Spanish explorers who first saw the armadillo gave it this name. Its skin has small scales made of hard bone. This creates the armor that covers it from its head to its tail.

Armadillos live in places with soft sand and soil. They dig in the ground to find food. They eat mostly insects and some plants and fruit. Armadillos use their sticky tongues to catch bugs. They have poor eyesight but use their good sense of smell to find food. Strong, curved claws and strong legs help them dig for the food. They also use their claws to dig burrows for homes.

An armadillo's armor is heavy, but it can swim when it needs to. It gulps air to help it float on water. Armadillos can also hold their breath for several minutes. The weight from their armor helps weigh them down so that they can walk along the bottom of rivers and streams.

One kind of armadillo can curl into a ball. This helps to protect it from predators. Other animals cannot eat the armadillo because only its hard outer shell is showing. This armadillo always has a safe hiding place.

Brave Knights

In medieval times, knights had to protect themselves. Swords were often used during battles. Knights would wear suits of armor and carry shields. Some suits were made of metal rings. Others were made from metal plates. Knights also wore helmets to protect their faces and heads.

Mail armor was made from thousands of tiny metal rings that were linked together. Worn like a long coat, mail was easy for a knight to move in. But, it could be pierced by an arrow or sword. Knights needed something else for protection.

Soon, knights began wearing metal plates of armor. This type of armor was heavier to wear. The rigid plates were hooked together with movable rivets and leather straps. These separate plates allowed a knight to move different parts of his body. This armor helped protect the knight from injury or death.

Knights often rode horses while in battle. These were known as warhorses. A knight would train his warhorse not to shy away from danger. Knights would also dress their horses in metal plates of armor. These were placed on a horse's neck, face, chest, and sides.

Knights used different weapons in battle. A lance was a long wooden pole with a sharp metal tip. It could be used while riding a horse. Swords had long, sharp blades with handles. Knights used swords when they were not on horseback. They carried shields to protect themselves from injuries from swords and lances. Knights were brave and skilled fighters who were always prepared to battle.

Name _____

Answer the questions.

1. Why did the author write "An Armored Animal"?

   _____

   _____

   _____

2. In "An Armored Animal," how do armadillos use their armor?

   A. to protect them from predators

   B. to keep them dry

   C. to help them run

   D. to help them find food

3. What is the main idea of "Brave Knights"?

   _____

   _____

   _____

4. In "Brave Knights," when did knights wear armor?

   A. when they were hunting

   B. when they were swimming

   C. when they were sleeping

   D. when they were in battle

5. In "Brave Knights," what was armor made from? What were its advantages?

   _____

   _____

   _____

   _____

Name _____

6. Complete the chart to compare information from both passages to tell what the armor is made from, how it provides protection, and how the animal or person moves with it on.

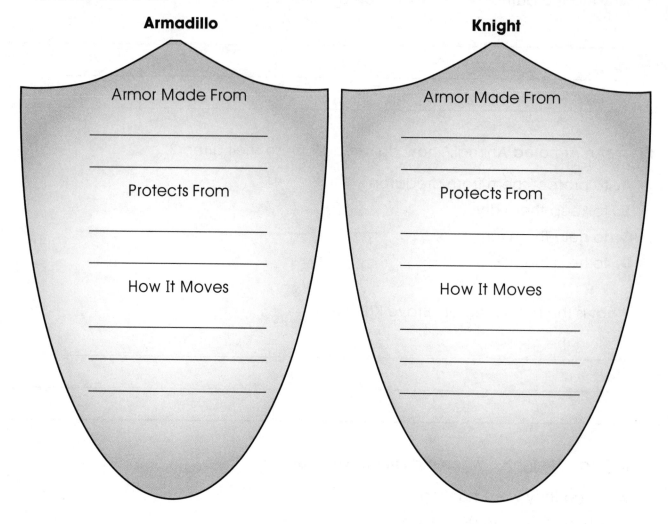

Armadillo

Armor Made From

_____

_____

Protects From

_____

_____

How It Moves

_____

_____

_____

Knight

Armor Made From

_____

_____

Protects From

_____

_____

How It Moves

_____

_____

_____

7. How does their armor help protect both the armadillo and a knight?

_____

_____

_____

_____

_____

_____

_____

48

An Incredible Journey

President Thomas Jefferson had an important job. He knew of land out west that had not yet been explored. He wanted a team of people to travel to the West. They would write about what the land looked like. They would also tell about the people they met. He chose Meriwether Lewis and William Clark to make the trip.

The explorers brought along others to help them. They packed canoes, tents, and food. Glass beads were brought to trade with people they met. They wrote in journals and drew pictures. They discovered many plants and animals that people back home had never seen. Grizzly bears and prairie dogs were animals that were new to them. They even took a prairie dog back with them.

The team was to travel until they reached the Pacific Ocean. They did not know what they would find along the way. They traveled across rivers. They climbed mountains. In the winter, they set up camps until the weather got warmer. The group covered many miles and had been traveling for over a year. After a long **journey**, the explorers finally reached the Pacific Ocean. The trip was a success! Winter was coming, and the weather was growing colder. The group set up camp until spring. Then, they would begin the trip home.

More than two years later, the team arrived home. People were surprised to see them. Many thought the explorers had died on the long and difficult journey. They were welcomed home as heroes.

Sacagawea

Meriwether Lewis and William Clark were asked to explore the land west of the Mississippi River. They needed others to join them on their **journey**. They asked 31 people to go with them. One additional traveler was Seaman, Lewis's large dog. Almost all of the explorers were men. Only one woman traveled with them. Her name was Sacagawea, and she was an American Indian. Lewis and Clark hoped Sacagawea could help them talk to other native tribes they would meet.

Lewis and Clark were not sure about having a woman travel with them. But, Sacagawea was a helpful guide. She knew the land they were going to explore. She helped them gather plants and find food to eat. When someone in the group got sick, she took care of them.

The group needed things that they did not bring with them. Sacagawea helped Lewis and Clark trade with native tribes to get these things. While on the trip, she gave birth to a baby boy. She carried him on her back in a special pouch. When tribes saw her and her baby, they knew the group would not hurt them.

Sacagawea helped Lewis and Clark get horses for travel and fur coats for winter. She also made it easier for them to travel on land owned by native tribes. Sacagawea spoke two native languages. Native people told her about trails the group should take to get to the Pacific Ocean.

Lewis and Clark wrote about how much Sacagawea helped them. Without her, the trip would not have been a success. She was a brave and helpful woman.

Name _____

Answer the questions.

1. Why did the author write "An Incredible Journey"?

   A. to teach readers about Lewis and Clark's exploration of the West

   B. to teach readers about animals found in the West

   C. to teach readers about American Indians

   D. to teach readers about Thomas Jefferson

2. According to "An Incredible Journey," what did Lewis and Clark **not** take when they started their journey?

   A. food

   B. canoes

   C. glass beads

   D. horses

3. As used in both texts, what does the word **journey** mean?

   _____

   _____

4. Write **true** or **false**.

   _____ Sacagawea carried her baby boy on the trip.

5. According to "Sacagawea," how did she help Lewis and Clark?

   _____

   _____

   _____

   _____

   _____

   _____

   _____

Name _____

6. Sacagawea, Lewis, and Clark each helped make the journey west a success. Using information from both passages, complete the Venn diagram.

Sacagawea   **Lewis and Clark**

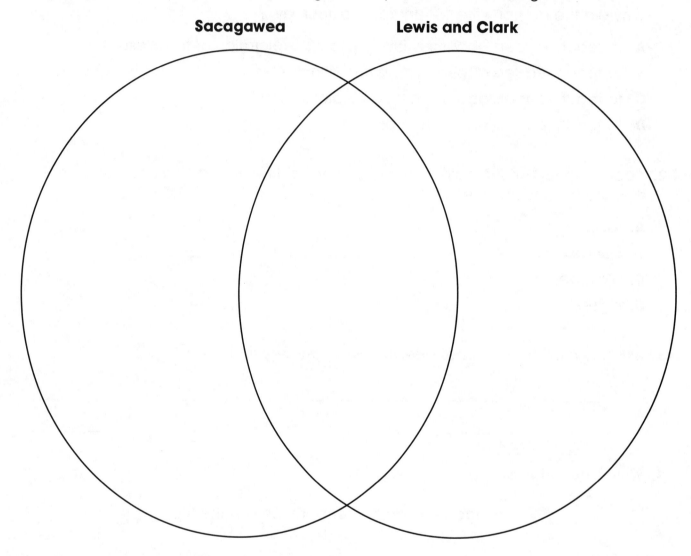

7. Write about how Sacagawea, Lewis, and Clark may have felt at various points on their journey.

_____

_____

_____

_____

_____

Smelling and the Nose

People use their noses to smell things. Your nose sends messages to your brain when a scent reaches it. Then, your brain tells you what the scent is that you are smelling. **Odors** are the scents your nose can detect.

Smells can remind us of certain things. When you smell cookies baking, it may make you feel hungry. It may remind you of your grandmother's kitchen. When you smell wood burning, you may be reminded of wintertime. The smell of cologne may make you think of your dad. The bad smell of burning toast tells you something is wrong. When you smell the strong odor of rotten food, your nose is warning you not to eat that food.

How does your nose help you smell? Inside your nose, there are millions of tiny hairs called cilia. These hairs are connected to smell sensors. When the cilia pick up a scent, these sensors send a message to your brain. Your brain identifies the scent.

Your sense of smell also helps you taste the food you eat. When you have a cold and get a stuffy nose, you will not be able to taste your food. The mucous in your nose keeps the cilia from picking up scents. Try this experiment next time you are about to eat something. Pinch your nose as you take a bite. Can you still taste it?

Tasting and the Tongue

Your tongue does many things for you. It helps you chew, speak, and swallow. It also helps naturally clean your teeth after eating. Your tongue guides food into your throat to prevent choking.

Your tongue is a large muscle attached to the bottom of your mouth. The top of it is covered with taste buds that have taste receptors. The taste buds tell you if you are eating something sweet, salty, sour, bitter, or savory. Every food you eat is a mixture of these five flavors. Because of taste buds, you can tell if you are eating sweet ice cream or salty pretzels. Your tongue also tells you about the texture and temperature of foods. You can tell if something is creamy, crunchy, hot, or cold.

But, it is not just your tongue that helps you taste your favorite foods. Your nose plays a part too. While you are chewing, the food in your mouth releases chemicals. These travel to your nose. Your taste buds and your nose work together to smell and taste what you put in your mouth.

Try giving your tongue a workout. Can you touch your nose with your tongue? Can you say the tongue twister "red leather, yellow leather" three times quickly? Eat something sweet while holding an onion slice under your nose. Was your tongue confused?

Name _____

Answer the questions.

1. What is the main idea of "Smelling and the Nose"?

   A. to teach readers about colds

   B. to teach readers how the nose helps a person smell

   C. to teach readers about odors

   D. to teach readers about being healthy

2. As used in "Smelling and the Nose," what does the word **odor** mean?

   A. perfume

   B. sweet

   C. stinky

   D. scent

3. According to "Smelling and the Nose," how does your nose help you smell scents?

   _____

   _____

   _____

4. According to "Tasting and the Tongue," what kind of body part is the tongue?

   A. a bone

   B. a muscle

   C. a taste bud

   D. an organ

5. Write **true** or **false**.

   _____ The tongue has taste buds.

Name _____

6. Complete the chart with details about the nose and the tongue. Read the passages again if you need help.

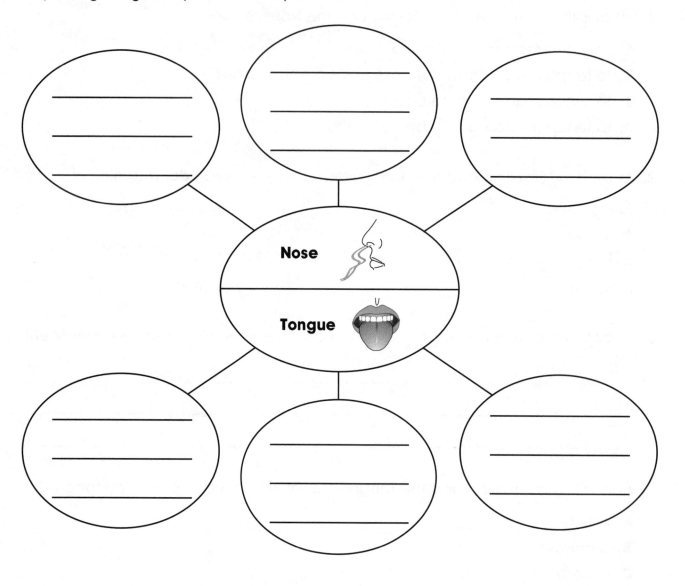

7. Compare the "jobs" of the nose and the tongue. How do they work together?

_____

_____

_____

_____

_____

_____

The Pony Express

How did people send letters over long distances before there were mail trucks and planes? The pony express was one way! The pony express carried mail about 2,000 miles (3,220 km) from the East to the West. It took about nine days to deliver a letter with the pony express. It would take a horse-drawn carriage several weeks to make the same trip. Before the pony express, mail was delivered to the west by ships.

Pony express riders traveled on horseback. They rode on a route with many stops. These stops were called stations. Riders would take turns carrying letters. The letters were placed in a special leather covering with four locking pockets. This was called a **mochila**. A water sack for the rider was also in the mochila. The mochila was thrown over the saddle. It was kept in place by the rider sitting on it. When a rider arrived at a station, he would change horses. The trip was long and riders rode through the day and night. Having stations meant that no one rider would have to make the entire trip.

The biggest problem for riders was the weather. They had to ride in the rain, snow, and wind. They had to ride through the mountains and across rivers. Sometimes, bandits would try to steal the mail from the riders. They used only the fastest horses so that they could travel quickly.

The pony express only lasted a short time, less than two years. A telegraph line connecting the East and the West was completed in 1861. Messages could be sent faster by telegraph. The pony express was no longer needed.

The US Post Office

Long before you could call, text, or email friends, you could mail letters. Long ago, it might take weeks for a letter to arrive. Getting a letter was very exciting!

Post offices used to be in taverns, or restaurants. These places gathered mail. Then, people would go there to pick up letters. Later, people would have their own mailboxes where their letters could be delivered. Soon, each city or town had a **postmaster**. This person worked to get the mail delivered to people's homes and businesses. The US Post Office was formed in 1775. It helped to connect all of the colonies that were scattered across the eastern United States.

Mail carriers started out delivering mail by walking, riding horses, and using rafts and rowboats. Today, only one place still gets its mail delivered by mule. It is an American Indian reservation at the bottom of the Grand Canyon. Trucks and cars cannot reach it. So, mules are used to carry the mail down a path into the canyon. It is a three-hour trip, one way, every day!

Later, mail would be delivered to post offices by trains or boats, such as fast-moving steamboats. Now, mail is delivered by plane or truck. At first, it took almost six weeks to mail a letter from the East to the West. Now, mail can be sent with overnight delivery. Millions of letters and packages are mailed all over the country every day.

Stamps are used to pay the postage for a letter to be mailed. People once had to use glue or paste to stick stamps on letters. Stamps today have self-stick backs. There are many kinds of postage stamps. Some stamp designs honor people or remember important events. Some designs highlight nature or celebrate holidays. Interesting stamps come from countries all over the world.

Name _____

Answer the questions.

1. What is the main idea of "The Pony Express"?

    A. to teach readers about one way that mail was delivered

    B. to teach readers about horses

    C. to teach readers about trains

    D. to teach readers about post offices

2. According to "The Pony Express," what was the biggest problem for riders?

    _____

    _____

    _____

3. As used in "The Pony Express," what does the word **mochila** mean?

    _____

    _____

4. According to "The US Post Office," what does a **postmaster** do?

    A. writes letters to people

    B. sorts out the mail

    C. sees that people get their mail

    D. designs stamps for letters

5. Write **true** or **false**.

    _____ People used to pick up their mail at taverns.

Name _____

6. Complete the Venn diagram to compare the information about mail delivery. Read the passages again if you need help.

Pony Express   **Post Office**

7. It has always been important to carry mail from place to place, even though it took time and was hard work. Why? Use information from the passages to support your answer.

_____

_____

_____

_____

_____

_____

The Grimke Sisters against Slavery

Sarah and Angelina Grimke grew up on a **plantation** in South Carolina. Their father provided well for his family. Slaves were trained to take care of their every need.

When Sarah was young she was given a slave as a gift. The slave helped her bathe and dress. Sarah's slave did whatever she was asked. She even slept on the floor outside Sarah's door at night.

Sarah was a kind girl. She started to hate slavery at a young age. She was upset that slaves were not allowed to go to school. She tried teaching her own slave to read in secret. They were caught by her father. Both girls were in trouble.

Angelina was younger than her sister Sarah. But, she was also against slavery. She saw some cruel things that happened to slaves. She saw a boy who could hardly walk. He had been beaten with a whip. Sometimes, her own family's slaves were mistreated.

When they were older, Angelina and Sarah went to Philadelphia. They made friends with people called **abolitionists**. The abolitionists wanted to end slavery. Angelina wrote a letter supporting their cause. She became well known because of it.

Angelina and Sarah traveled all over speaking out against slavery. Angelina did most of the speaking. Sarah wrote letters and articles that were read by many people.

At one time, the sisters had been waited on by slaves. Now, they washed their own clothes. They cooked their own meals. They worked hard so that slaves would be treated like others.

Riding the Underground Railroad

The Underground Railroad was not underground. It had nothing to do with trains. It was the name of a group of people who helped slaves escape from the South. They helped them find their way to freedom. They helped them travel to the northern states.

Railroad names were used as codes. A "conductor" was the person who led the slaves north. Safe stops along the way were called "stations" and "depots." The stations were run by "stationmasters." "Stockholders" helped by donating money, food, or clothing.

It was not easy to escape the **plantation** if you were a slave. Slaves were closely watched. They had little money. They had to walk from place to place. They could easily be seen. The best escape plan was to join with a conductor and other slaves.

Conductors sometimes came right onto the plantation. They made their plans in secret. Once off the plantation, slaves were given new clothes so that they would not stand out. Most of the travel was at night. The conductors led slaves from one station to another. The slaves rested and ate at each station.

The Underground Railroad was made up of many people who hated slavery. Conductors and stationmasters were both white and black. They all risked their lives to help slaves escape. Harriet Tubman, one of the best-known conductors, lived in the North. She was a freed slave who made many dangerous trips into the South. She brought many slaves to freedom.

Name _____

Answer the questions.

1. What is the main idea of the first paragraph in "The Grimke Sisters against Slavery"?

_____

_____

2. What is the main idea of the first paragraph of "Riding the Underground Railroad"?

_____

_____

3. What was the author's purpose in writing "The Grimke Sisters against Slavery"?

_____

_____

4. What was the author's purpose in writing "Riding the Underground Railroad"?

_____

_____

5. As used in both texts, what does the word **plantation** mean?

_____

_____

6. As used in "The Grimke Sisters against Slavery," what does the word **abolitionist** mean?

_____

_____

7. Characters in each passage fought against slavery. Complete the chart to compare what they did. Read the passages again if you need help.

	At first,	Then,	Finally,
The Grimke Sisters against Slavery			
Riding the Underground Railroad			

8. What did the two passages have in common?

_____

_____

_____

9. How were the two passages different?

_____

_____

_____

Farm Garden

Dear Emily,

Thank you for writing to me. You had questions about what it was like to live on a farm. I can imagine that living in an apartment building in a big city is very different from a farm!

It is springtime now, and we are getting ready to seed the fields for our crops. We will plant squash, tomatoes, cucumbers, and peppers. We also grow strawberries and blueberries.

To get the ground ready for planting we **till**, or break up, the soil. Then, seeds are planted in the ground. Some of the plants have been growing in the greenhouse. This lets us start growing plants when it is still too cold outside. When the plants are big enough, they will be planted in the field. We have a lot of plants to water. Luckily, there is a stream beside our fields where we get water for the crops. All of the crops need lots of water during the hot summer.

Soon, the crops will be ready to harvest. My family has workers that help pick the crops. After the crops are picked, they are washed and packed in baskets. We keep some for our family but sell most of what we grow. My favorite thing is helping to can fruits and vegetables to enjoy during the cold winter.

Good luck with your garden!

Your friend,

Sarah

Garden in the City

Dear Sarah,

I was so excited to get your letter! I love many things about living in a city. But, I do wish I could have a garden. I visit my grandparents often, and I always like helping them in their garden.

The last time my grandparents visited, they surprised me with a garden box. The best part about it is that I can keep it inside. I have the perfect sunny window to place it in. The box is made of wood. I covered the bottom of the box with plastic. Then, I put in some pebbles to help the water drain. Next, I added a layer of soil. Last, I sprinkled in some fertilizer.

We headed to the garden center to find some plants and seeds. I decided to buy tomato plants and pepper seeds. I could not wait to get home and add them to the garden! I carefully placed the tomato plants in the garden. I did not want to break the roots or leaves. Then, I planted the pepper seeds. I use a watering can to water my garden every day.

After a few weeks, the tiny pepper seedlings are beginning to poke through the soil! I am looking forward to eating the vegetables I have grown. And, the best part is, there are no weeds to pull!

Your friend,

Emily

Name _____

Answer the questions.

1. What does "Farm Garden" tell readers?

_____

_____

2. Number the steps to show how crops were grown in "Farm Garden."

_____ Water the crops.

_____ Plant the seeds.

_____ Till the soil.

_____ Pick the crops.

3. As used in "Farm Garden," what does the word **till** mean?

A. to break up   **B.** to water   **C.** to plant   **D.** to pick

4. What is the main idea of "Garden in the City"?

_____

_____

_____

5. In "Garden in the City," where did Emily put her garden box?

A. outside on the porch

B. in a sunny window

C. on a farm

D. at a park

6. In "Garden in the City," what did Emily do first to prepare her garden box?

A. Plastic was placed in the box.

B. Plants and seeds were added to the soil.

C. Soil was added to the box.

D. Pebbles were placed in the box.

Name _____

7. Complete the chart to show the steps for planting each garden. Read the passages again if you need help.

Farm Garden   **City Garden**

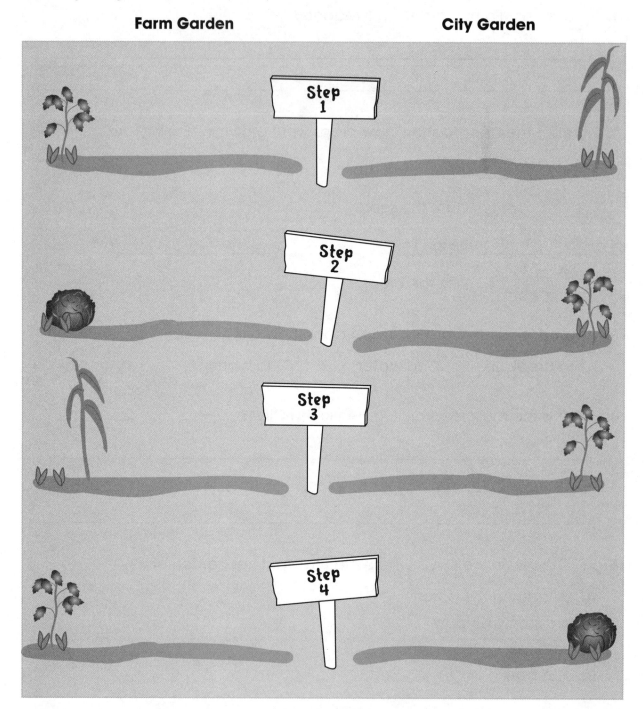

8. How are a city and a farm garden different? Name the advantages of each.

_____

_____

_____

_____

Mexico

Dear Classmates,

I am enjoying living in Mexico. My family and I have traveled to many different cities. I really like traveling to new places and meeting new people.

It took me a while to get used to going to school here. Everything is taught in Spanish. I knew a little Spanish when we got here. But at first, I could not understand most of what my teachers were saying. Now, I am doing much better and have no trouble with Spanish.

My school is large, so we go to school in shifts. One group of students goes to school in the morning and the other goes in the afternoon. My school also has uniforms that we wear every day.

My school is close to the ocean. I have learned how to surf since living here. Most days, I surf after school. One day, my family went snorkeling! I saw all kinds of colorful fish and coral. I have learned a new game called **loteria**. It is played with picture cards. It reminds me of bingo. At recess, we jump rope and play games like basketball.

I have tried some new foods. My favorite is mole. It is sauce made from peppers and spices. It is delicious! I have been practicing making it myself. I also like tamales. They are made of corn dough stuffed with meat or cheese. They are served steamed in a corn husk.

Adiós!

Rose

PS: Here, they call me "Rosa"!

Switzerland

Hello Friends,

Moving to Switzerland was a big change for my family and me. I miss my family and friends from home. But, I really love the beautiful country. We have visited the mountains and some of the many lakes that are here.

At school, we take a lot of field trips. Sometimes, we are away for several days and stay overnight. It's fun not to be in a classroom all of the time. We do not have school buses where I live. My brother and I walk to school every day. Children from our neighborhood walk with us.

We are close to many countries here. I have visited France and Italy. I hope to see Germany soon. People here speak all different languages. But, most people speak English too. I am learning to speak French and German, but I still have a lot to learn.

Every year there is a festival here. It is called **Fasnacht**. There is a parade where people dress up. I loved seeing all of the unique costumes. Performers throw candy to people lined up along the streets. Lanterns light up the sky at night. There are a lot of good foods to eat.

It was hard leaving my friends back home, but I am glad I came here. Maybe you could come visit me here one day. I hope you will like it as much as I do!

Your friend,

Allison

Name _____

Answer the questions.

1. What was the author's purpose in writing "Mexico"?

_____

_____

_____

2. As used in "Mexico," what does the word **loteria** mean?

    A. a book

    B. a game

    C. a TV show

    D. a city

3. Write about two things the author did in "Mexico."

_____

_____

_____

4. What is the main idea of "Mexico"?

_____

_____

_____

5. Write about two things the author did in "Switzerland."

_____

_____

_____

6. As used in "Switzerland," what does the word **Fasnacht** refer to?

    A. a play   **B.** a festival   **C.** a school   **D.** a mountain

Name _____

7. Complete the Venn diagram to compare the experiences the authors had in the countries they moved to. Read the passages again if you need help.

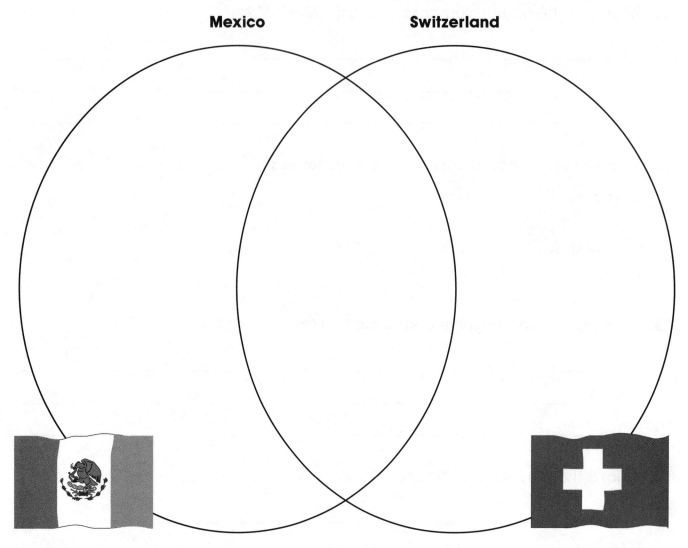

Mexico   Switzerland

8. Tell how each author felt about moving to a new place to live. What are things the authors had in common?

_____

_____

_____

_____

_____

_____

_____

Rocky

My name is John, and I love dogs. I wanted to do something to help people and animals. I decided to help train a dog to become a guide dog. Guide dogs help people who are blind. Guide dogs act as eyes for people who cannot see.

I was so excited the day our dog Rocky came to our house! He was just a few weeks old and still a puppy. He did not sleep much at night. He needed to go outside a lot. My job was to feed, walk, and groom Rocky.

Rocky has to wear a special harness with a handle that the person he will be helping can hold. Rocky needed to learn not to be distracted by the things around him. I practice walking him while my sister talks to him. She also tries to give him treats. At first, Rocky would go over to her and wag his tail. But, after many hours of practice, he now stays with me and keeps walking. Rocky is very smart and learns things quickly.

Rocky needs to stay with me most of the day. He comes with me to the store and the library. Since Rocky will be a guide dog, he is allowed to go where other dogs are not. This will help him learn to be with his **handler**, or the person he will be helping. He will need to spend almost all of his time guiding his handler.

Soon, Rocky will go to live with another person who will teach him commands. I will certainly miss Rocky, but I am so happy he will have a very special job.

Our Dog Maggie

My family loves to explore the woods and go hiking. We always take our dog Maggie along. She is a big dog and full of energy. She loves running and being outdoors.

Last Saturday, we decided to go hiking at a park near our house. I packed a bag with supplies, including water for Maggie. It was a hot day, and I knew we would be gone a long time.

Maggie knows the commands "come" and "stay." She will run to us and stay still when she hears my parents or me calling out to her. We had almost finished our hike when I heard Maggie barking very loudly on the trail ahead. My dad called "come," but Maggie did not move. She kept barking. As we got closer, we saw a bee's nest lying on the ground. There were many bees swarming around the hive. We slowly and carefully walked past the hive. We made sure to stay as far away as possible.

When we got home, I noticed Maggie's foot was very swollen. The vet said she had been stung by a bee. He gave her medicine to help her feel better. Maggie was brave to warn us about the danger ahead.

Name _____

Answer the questions.

1. In "Rocky," what is the dog being trained to do?

_____

_____

2. As used in "Rocky," what does the word **handler** mean?

    A. a special leash

    B. a guide dog

    C. a dog collar

    D. a person who uses a guide dog

3. Write **true** or **false**.

    _____ A guide dog is easily distracted.

4. What is the main idea of "Our Dog Maggie"?

_____

_____

_____

5. In "Our Dog Maggie," what did Maggie do to protect her family?

_____

_____

_____

6. What word did the author use to describe her dog in "Our Dog Maggie"?

    A. afraid

    B. disobedient

    C. brave

    D. funny

Name _____

7. Complete the Venn diagram to compare the dogs in "Rocky" and "Our Dog Maggie."

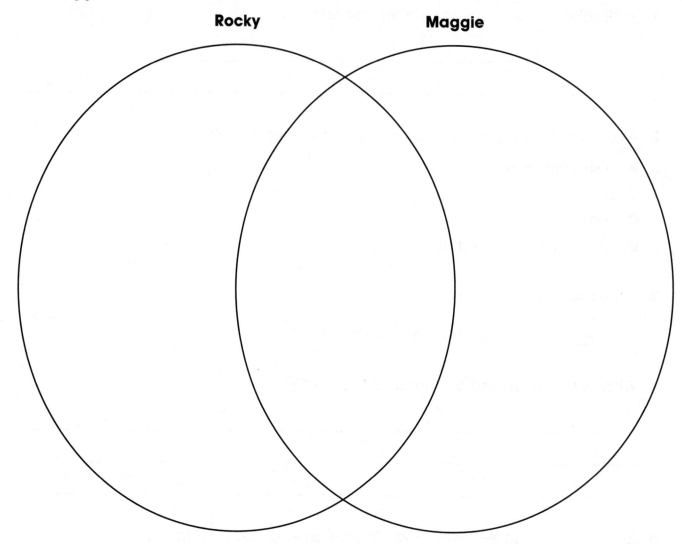

Rocky   **Maggie**

8. What did both dogs do to help people? Use adjectives to describe each dog in your writing.

_____

_____

_____

_____

_____

_____

_____

A Life on the Ocean Wave
By Epes Sargent

A life on the ocean wave,
A home on the rolling deep,
Where the scattered waters rave,
And the winds their revels keep!
Like an eagle caged, I pine
On this dull, unchanging shore:
Oh! give me the flashing brine,
The spray and the tempest's roar!

Once more on the deck I stand
Of my own swift-gliding craft:
Set sail! Farewell to the land!
The gale follows fair abaft.
We shoot through the sparkling foam
Like an ocean-bird, set free;
Like the ocean-bird, our home
We'll find far out on the sea.

The land is no longer in view,
The clouds have begun to frown;
But with a stout vessel and crew,
We'll say, Let the storm come down!
And the song of our hearts shall be,
While the winds and waters rave,
A home on the rolling sea!
A life on the ocean wave!

On a Stormy Day

As I play on the shore, I can see the storm clouds coming in. They are dark and far off now, but soon they will be here. The wind is picking up. Kelp and other kinds of seaweed tumble across the sand. The waves are crashing. I watch the seagulls bobbing up and down in the water. They look like they are enjoying the bumpy ride!

As the sand starts to blow in swirls, I turn my back to the wind. It's strange how just minutes ago, it was calm and bright. The clouds are rolling in closer now. I know I should soon be on my way home. But, I want to stay and see just what this storm will bring.

As I look out over the water, I see a boat moving toward shore. The captain knows a storm is coming, and it's best not to be adrift. I watch as it floats up and down, moving closer and closer to land like a bouncing ball that's not sure where to land.

I can feel the spray of the waves as I prepare to leave. The sand castle I made today is now part of the sea. I wonder if other sea creatures know what is happening on this beautiful beach. Maybe they are safe inside their ocean homes beneath these wild waves. I should be there too, and soon I will leave the shore. But for now, I am content to enjoy the salty air and listen to the sounds of a lively seashore.

Just as fast as the storm began, it soon begins to fade. The waves are calmer now and the sun breaks through the clouds like an egg coming out of its shell. The sky begins to brighten, and I can feel its warm rays on my face. Suddenly, it seems perfect to stay and enjoy the waves for a little longer. I will dive back into the water in a while. My underwater home seems far away at this moment.

Name _____

Answer the questions.

I. In "A Life on the Ocean Wave," what is happening in the poem?

_____

_____

2. What genre is "A Life on the Ocean Wave"? How do you know?

_____

_____

3. Is "On a Stormy Day" fiction or nonfiction? Explain your answer.

_____

_____

4. What made the narrator think about leaving the beach in "On a Stormy Day?"

_____

_____

5. What words or phrases in "On a Stormy Day" tell the reader a storm is coming?

_____

_____

6. What imagery did the author use in "On a Stormy Day" to describe the sun breaking through the clouds?

   A. like a ball bouncing without knowing where to land

   B. like sea creatures hiding in their shells

   C. like an egg coming out of its shell

   D. like an eagle trapped in a cage

Name _____

7. Describe the sights, sounds, and feelings the storm conveyed in each passage.

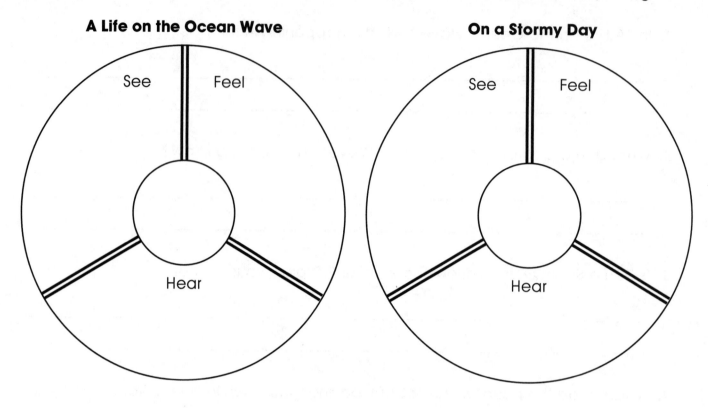

A Life on the Ocean Wave

See | Feel
Hear

On a Stormy Day

See | Feel
Hear

8. Write about how the storm was an important element in each passage.

_____
_____
_____
_____
_____
_____
_____
_____
_____
_____
_____

The Wind and the Moon
by George MacDonald (excerpted)

Said the Wind to the Moon,
"I will blow you out;
You stare
In the air
Like a ghost in a chair,
Always looking what I am about—
I hate to be watched;
I'll blow you out."

The Wind blew hard,
and out went the Moon.
So, deep
On a heap
Of clouds to sleep,
Down lay the Wind, and slumbered soon,
Muttering low,
"I've done that for the Moon."

He turned in his bed;
she was there again!
On high
In the sky,
With her one ghost eye,
The Moon shone white and alive and plain.
Said the Wind,
"I will blow you out again."

The Wind blew hard,
and the Moon grew dim.
"With my sledge,
And my wedge,
I have knocked off her edge!
If only I blow right fierce and grim,
The creature will soon be
dimmer than dim."

Said the Wind:
"What a marvel of power I am
With my breath,
Good faith!
I blew her to death—
First blew her away right out of the sky—
Then blew her in;
what strength have I!"

But the Moon
she knew nothing about the affair;
For high
In the sky,
With her one white eye,
Motionless, miles above the air,
She had never heard
the great Wind blare.

The Legend of the Moon
A Legend of the Cree

A long time ago, there was no moon. Only the sun was in the sky. The creator of the sun had asked a man and his two children to live in the sky. The man was to keep the sun's fire burning. All three lived peacefully together.

It was the girl's job to keep their home neat. When she shook out the fluffy blankets, the feathers would fall to the earth as snow. It was the boy's job to hunt and fish. When he hung his nets out to dry, droplets of water fell to the earth as rain. They worked all day while their father was away keeping the sun's fire burning bright.

But, the man was growing old and soon it would be up to his children to care for the sun. When that day came, the children mourned their father. But, the next morning, it was time to tend the sun again. The children began to **quarrel** over who would do the task.

"I should tend the fire because I am older," the girl said.

"I am the man, and I should tend the fire," the boy said. They continued yelling and arguing for a long time.

The people on Earth were anxious and wondered why the sun had not risen. So, the creator went back to the sky to resolve the problem. When he arrived, he heard the children quarreling.

He angrily told the boy, "You will tend the sun's fire." He told the girl, "You will work just as hard as your brother, but you will tend fire in another place. You will work at night and be known as the moon. And as punishment, you will only see each other from across the sky."

And it remains so even today.

Name _____

Answer the questions.

I. Is "The Wind and the Moon" fiction or nonfiction? How do you know?

_____

_____

2. What was the wind trying to do in "The Wind and the Moon"? Why?

_____

_____

3. In "The Wind and the Moon," was the wind actually blowing the moon from the sky? How do you know?

_____

_____

4. Is "The Legend of the Moon" fiction or nonfiction? How do you know?

_____

_____

5. As used in "The Legend of the Moon," what does the word **quarrel** mean?

    A. to agree

    B. to laugh

    C. to share

    D. to argue

6. According to "The Legend of the Moon," what was the children's punishment?

_____

_____

Name _____

7. Complete the organizer to compare the story elements in each passage. Read the passages again if you need help.

	The Wind and the Moon	**The Legend of the Moon**
Main Idea		
Characters		
Problem		
Solution		

8. Write about the role the moon played in each passage.

_____

_____

_____

_____

_____

How the Chipmunk Got Her Stripes
A Legend of the Iroquois

At one time, Earth was covered in darkness. None of the animals that lived there had ever seen daylight.

One day, Bear, the leader of the animals, gathered them all in the forest. They talked about whether they should stay in the darkness or if they should also have light. Bear and the other creatures decided to climb the highest mountain. There were no trees on the mountaintop, and the stars were shining brightly in the sky. There, Bear told them the darkness was better. All of the animals could sleep better in the dark. Raccoon wanted the darkness too. He was smart enough to find food even in the dark.

But, Chipmunk did not agree. She thought it was best to have both light and dark. Bear and Chipmunk continued to argue. They could not agree about what to do.

Bear and the other creatures grew tired, but Chipmunk kept talking. As the other animals fell asleep, Chipmunk still kept talking. Eventually, the sun came up in the sky, and the animals saw light for the first time. They were amazed.

Chipmunk was so excited that she began dancing around. Bear was angry that he had not gotten his way. He chased Chipmunk all of the way down the mountain. Just as Chipmunk was almost safely away, Bear stretched out his paw and scratched Chipmunk's back. And that is why Chipmunk has stripes on her back to this day.

The Missing Strawberry

Juan loved strawberries. So, when Juan saw strawberry plants at the garden store, he really wanted one. Finally, his dad agreed to buy a strawberry plant. But, he said that Juan would have to plant, water, and weed it.

Juan knew strawberries needed lots of sun and water. He found the perfect spot in their backyard. He raked up the soil and planted his strawberry plant. At first, the plant was just a tiny sprout, but after several weeks, it began growing bigger and bigger. Soon, Juan noticed small flowers on the plant. "These will grow into strawberries," he thought.

Every day, Juan tended his strawberry plant. One day, he was carefully pulling weeds. He saw a small animal running away quickly. He was not sure what it was. So, he kept working.

After a few weeks, Juan saw a green strawberry on the plant. His dad told him it needed to ripen before being picked. Juan was anxious. He really wanted a juicy strawberry!

Finally, the strawberry was red and ripe. Juan went out to the backyard. There was the plant, but where was the strawberry? He looked all around, but it was not there. Just then, Juan saw the small animal he had seen before. It **scurried** away with a special treat. It had picked the strawberry from Juan's plant. What a clever little chipmunk!

Name _____

Answer the questions.

I. Is "How the Chipmunk Got Her Stripes" fiction or nonfiction? How do you know?

_____

_____

2. According to "How the Chipmunk Got Her Stripes," why did Bear get angry at Chipmunk?

_____

_____

3. In "How the Chipmunk Got Her Stripes," which animal wanted to stay in the dark?

   A. Deer

   B. Bear

   C. Chipmunk

   D. Rabbit

4. Is "The Missing Strawberry" fiction or nonfiction? How do you know?

_____

_____

5. In "The Missing Strawberry," what did Juan see on the plant before the strawberry grew?

   A. bugs

   B. flowers

   C. chipmunks

   D. leaves

6. As used in "The Missing Strawberry," what does the word **scurried** mean?

   A. laughed

   B. picked

   C. jumped

   D. hurried

Name _____

7. Complete the organizer to compare details about the chipmunks in each passage. Read the passages again if you need help.

How the Chipmunk Got Her Stripes   **The Missing Strawberry**

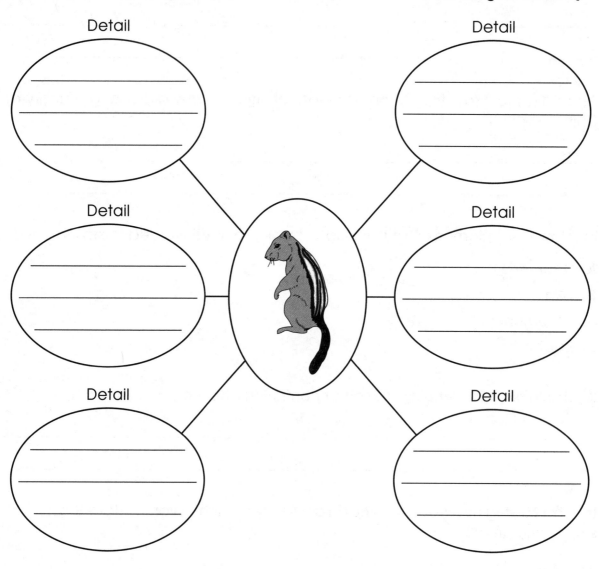

Detail

Detail

Detail

Detail

Detail

Detail

8. Compare the lessons or morals in the two passages.

_____

_____

_____

_____

_____

My Shadow
by Robert Louis Stevenson

I have a little shadow that goes in and out with me,
And what can be the use of him is more than I can see.
He is very, very like me from the heels up to the head;
And I see him jump before me, when I jump into my bed.

The funniest thing about him is the way he likes to grow—
Not at all like proper children, which is always very slow;
For he sometimes shoots up taller like an India-rubber ball,
And he sometimes gets so little that there's none of him at all.

He hasn't got a notion of how children ought to play,
And can only make a fool of me in every sort of way.
He stays so close behind me, he's a coward you can see;
I'd think shame to stick to nursie as that shadow sticks to me!

One morning, very early, before the sun was up,
I rose and found the shining dew on every buttercup;
But my lazy little shadow, like an arrant sleepy-head,
Had stayed at home behind me and was fast asleep in bed.

The Dog Who Barks at Shadows

Dear Dog's Best Friend,

I sure hope you can help me with my best friend, my dog Toby. I got Toby when he was only two months old. We rescued him from a shelter.

When we first brought him home, Toby was very quiet. I think he was on his best behavior because he didn't want to go back to the shelter. We played together all summer long, and soon he started to trust us. He started acting more like a dog!

But, ever since I went back to school, Toby has developed an annoying habit. My mom says it is because he misses me. It doesn't matter where Toby is or what he is doing. He can't stop staring at shadows. Even worse, he barks at them all! He looks out the window, sees shadows of trees or the house, whatever—and barks! He barks at his shadow and my shadow, in the house or outside.

Mom says his barking is sending her around the bend. So, I have to figure out how to stop Toby from barking at shadows. Can you help?

Your friend,

Gabe

Dear Gabe,

Thank you for rescuing a dog from the shelter! I can tell that you will make a responsible dog owner.

Sometimes, dogs bark because they are afraid. Sometimes, it is because they are bored and don't have enough to do.

Since this problem started when you went back to school, my guess is that Toby does not have enough to do. You probably played with him a lot during the summer.

I think Toby is bored. Get up early and take him for a long walk. Run with him. Then, when you get home from school, take him for another jog. Get Toby a backpack and take along bottles of water and a flying disk. Stop along the way to drink water. Toss the flying disk for a while.

Keep Toby busy. A busy and tired dog is a happy dog. He will soon forget about all of the shadows!

Good luck,

The Dog's Best Friend

Name _____

Answer the questions.

1. Is "My Shadow" fiction or nonfiction? How do you know?

_____

_____

2. What genre is "My Shadow"? How do you know?

_____

_____

3. Is "The Dog Who Barks at Shadows" fiction or nonfiction? How do you know?

_____

_____

4. What genre is "The Dog Who Barks at Shadows"? How do you know?

_____

_____

5. Why do you think the boy in "My Shadow" thinks the way the shadow grows is odd?

   A. The shadow grows slowly.

   B. The shadow is sometimes tall and sometimes little.

   C. The shadow is like an India-rubber ball.

   D. The shadow is not like him at all.

6. In "The Dog Who Barks at Shadows," what clue helped the Dog's Best Friend figure out the problem?

   A. The dog barks at shadows all of the time.

   B. Gabe's mother says Toby's barking is sending her around the bend.

   C. Gabe said that Toby's barking started after he went back to school.

   D. Toby looks out of the windows too much.

Name _____

7. Complete the organizer to show how the authors used the idea of a shadow to tell about something else. Read the passages again if you need help.

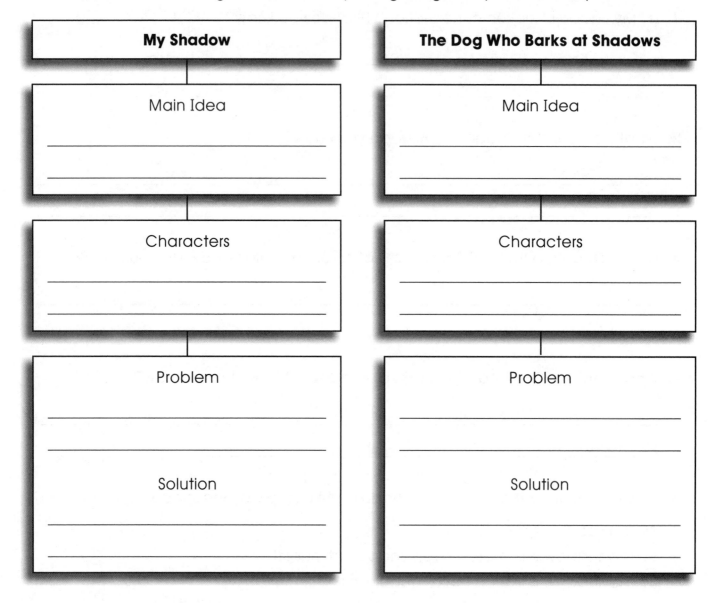

| **My Shadow** | **The Dog Who Barks at Shadows** |

Main Idea	Main Idea
_____	_____
_____	_____

Characters	Characters
_____	_____
_____	_____

Problem	Problem
_____	_____
_____	_____
Solution	Solution
_____	_____
_____	_____

8. How do shadows become the central figures in each passage?

_____

_____

_____

_____

_____

Answer Key

Pages 7–8

1. C; 2. A; 3. B; 4. D; 5. C; 6. Answers will vary but should include details from the passage such as (Physical Features) "The Ants and the Grasshopper"—late autumn, warm sunshine; "Ant Farmers"—clear paths for walking, climb trees and plants, large nest, underground garden; (Community Features) "The Ants and the Grasshopper"—family, work together, store up food in the summer; "Ant Farmers"—march in long lines carrying leaves, each has a job, live together; 7. Answers will vary but should include details comparing the passages and show an understanding of how ants work together to provide food for the entire community.

Pages 11–12

1. A; 2. A; 3. Answers will vary but should include ideas such as pioneers traveled in covered wagons to find new homes, and the journey was long and dangerous. 4. true; 5. B; 6. Answers will vary but should include details from the passage such as (Travel) Pioneer Times—wagon, horseback, walk; Today—car, bike, bus, airplane; (Getting Food) Pioneer Times—hunted, gathered, farmed; Today—shop, garden (Chores) Pioneer Times—getting water, watching children, cooking meals; Today—cleaning room, homework, watching children; 7. Answers will vary but should include details comparing both passages and show an understanding of how pioneers had a difficult and often dangerous journey and had to work daily to get water and food.

Pages 15–16

1. Answers will vary but should include information such as the settlers wanted to farm the land the tribes lived on. The US government passed a law saying they had to leave. 2. Answers will vary but should include wanting to tell the story of the Cherokee's forced march. 3. false; 4. A; 5. C; 6. D; 7. Answers will vary but should include details from the passage such as (First) Cherokee lived on their own land. (Next) Settlers wanted the land. (Last) Cherokee were forced to walk to Oklahoma. 8. Answers will vary but should include details comparing both passages and show an understanding of how the Cherokee were treated poorly and forced to leave against their will, creating suffering, sadness, and fear.

Pages 19–20

1. C; 2. C; 3. Answers will vary but should include information from the passage such as both fear and gratitude for being safe and together. 4. B; 5. studies earthquakes; 6. Answers will vary but should include ("The San Francisco Earthquake") First, Earth's plates moved. Next, buildings fell and fires started. Finally, the city was mostly destroyed and people lived in tents for weeks. ("The Day the City Shook") First, the author woke up when the room was shaking. Next, he and his family escaped outdoors. Finally, they lived in a tent and cooked on a brick stove. 7. Answers will vary but should include details from the passage such as the earthquake destroyed homes and buildings in the city, fires burned for days, and people had no homes, food, or water.

Pages 23–24

1. sunlight and water or rain; 2. B; 3. red, orange, yellow, green, blue, indigo, and violet; 4. B; 5. A; 6. Answers will vary but should include ("Colors in the Sky") How—Sunlight and water combine to form a rainbow. What—sunlight and rain or water; ("Painting a Rainbow") How—The birds dipped their wings in the paint and flew across the sky painting a rainbow. What—jars of paint and flying birds; 7. "Colors in the Sky." Answers will vary but should include logical reasoning about the difference between fact and fiction.

Pages 27–28

1. a singing contest; 2. C; 3. Answers will vary but should include wanting to tell readers about a legend involving dolphins. 4. Answers will vary but should include sharing information about how dolphins have been known to help humans. 5. A; 6. B; 7. "Friends in the Sea" (Main Idea) Dolphins have been known to rescue and help people in the ocean. (Characters) dolphins and people; (Problem) Divers got stranded in the ocean. Swimmers were threatened by a shark. (Solution) Dolphins gathered around the divers to keep them safe. They leaped out of the water to guide rescue boats. Dolphins herded the people together and slapped their tails on the water until the shark left. "Arion" (Main Idea) Your special talents may have more worth than you realize. (Characters) Arion, King, Sailors, Townspeople; (Problem) Sailors tried to steal Arion's gold and jewels and pushed him overboard. (Solution) A dolphin carried Arion home on its back. 8. Answers will vary

Answer Key

but should include facts from the passage. Answers will vary but may include that dolphins seem to be compassionate and have a history of helping and befriending people.

Pages 31–32
1. Answers will vary but should include when the tide comes in, pools of water collect among rocks and in the sand. When the tide recedes, the water is left. 2. A; 3. Answers will vary but should include informing readers about how tide pools are formed and what creatures live in them. 4. Answers will vary but should include sharing information on how to explore a tide pool without harming the creatures, what lives in a tide pool, and where to find tide pools. 5. D; 6. Answers will vary but could include marine algae, seaweed, mussels, oysters, crabs, sea stars, sea urchins, sand dollars, and barnacles. 7. (Attaches to Rocks) mussels, barnacles, (Lives under Rocks or Plants) sea urchin, sea star, crab, shrimp, oyster, (Lives inside a Shell) oyster, mussel, (Floats in Water) seaweed, marine algae; 8. Answers will vary but should include walk carefully, put back rocks and plants that you move, and do not take the creatures home as pets.

Pages 35–36
1. protecting the cattle herd; 2. C; 3. Answers will vary but should include informing readers about how cowboys lived and how they worked. 4. true; 5. D; 6. Answers will vary but could include keeping cattle together, guiding them on the trail, herding them to food and water, and protecting cattle from predators and rustlers.

7. Answers will vary but should include (Work) guiding cattle to food and water, protecting cattle, keeping cattle safe; (Clothing) jeans, leather chaps, hats with brims, neckerchiefs; (Food) beans, coffee, biscuits; 8. Answers will vary but should include working outside in hot and dusty weather, sleeping outside, protecting cattle from dangerous animals or rustlers, having little food and water, and the hard work of herding the cattle.

Pages 39–40
1. B; 2. Answers will vary but should include how the plant traps insects in its leaves, the leaves shut, and the insects cannot escape. 3. D; 4. B; 5. 2, 3, 1; 6. Answers will vary but should include ("Trap-Door Spider") digs a hole, hides behind door; ("Venus Flytrap") uses leaves to trap an insect inside; (Both) catch insects to eat, move quickly to capture a meal; 7. Answers will vary but should include that insects offer nutrients that the Venus flytrap does not get from the poor soil. The trap-door spider uses camouflage to hide its trap from prey.

Pages 43–44
1. Answers will vary but should include the first powered flying machine that could safely carry people. 2. A; 3. Answers will vary but should include that he was the first person to walk on the moon. 4. C; 5. true; 6. Answers will vary but should include (Neil Armstrong) Traveling Machine—Apollo 11 spacecraft; First To—walk on the moon; (Wright Brothers) Traveling Machine—an airplane; First To—fly in an airplane;

7. Answers will vary but should include how they were the first to fly in the air and to the moon. People fly in airplanes and astronauts fly in spacecraft because of their accomplishments.

Pages 47–48
1. Answers will vary but should include to inform readers about the armadillo. 2. A; 3. Answers will vary but should include that knights wore armor and carried weapons to protect themselves and their horses in battle. 4. D; 5. metal, Answers will vary. 6. Answers will vary but could include (Armadillos) Armor Made From—bones;Protects From—predators; How It Moves—walking, climbing, swimming; (Knight) Armor Made From—metal plates that move with them, Protects From—enemies; How It Moves—walking, riding on horseback; 7. Answers will vary but should include that the armor is a tough outer covering that helps protect them from enemies that might harm them.

Pages 51–52
1. A; 2. D; 3. Journey means a long trip. 4. true; 5. Sacagawea spoke native languages and helped Lewis and Clark talk to and trade with tribes. She helped them find food. She took care of people who were sick, and she guided them on trails she knew. 6. (Sacagawea) talked to tribes, guided the group on trails; (Lewis and Clark) wrote in journals to record explorations, discovered plants and animals, planned the journey; (Both) went on the journey, returned home safely; 7. Answers will vary but should include how they feared traveling to a new place, were

Answer Key

afraid they might face hostile tribes, worried they might not have enough food, and were excited to be going somewhere few had been.

Pages 55–56
1. B; 2. D; 3. The nose has tiny hairs called cilia that trap scents. These cilia send messages to the brain about what the smell could be. 4. B; 5. true; 6. Answers will vary but could include details such as (Nose) uses cilia to pick up scents, sends messages to the brain, and helps you taste foods; (Tongue) is a muscle, uses taste buds to send messages to the brain, can tell different textures apart, and helps you chew, swallow, and speak; 7. Answers will vary but should include how the nose detects odors and scents. These can protect you from danger by alerting you to a bad or dangerous smell. The tongue helps with taste, chewing, speaking, and swallowing. It prevents choking by guiding food into your throat.

Pages 59–60
1. A; 2. They had to ride in all kinds of weather. 3. a special leather covering with pockets to carry letters on horseback; 4. C; 5. true; 6. (Pony Express) used horses to deliver mail to special mail stations; (Post Office) uses trucks and planes to deliver mail to post offices, uses carriers to bring mail to homes and businesses with mailboxes; (Both) deliver mail to people; 7. Answers will vary but should include that people lived far away from each other and could not send news without sending letters. Letters were a way to get important information to people and to stay connected to others.

Pages 63–64
1. Sarah and Angelina Grimke grew up in a household where slaves did a lot of the work. 2. The Underground Railroad was a group of people who helped slaves escape to freedom in the North. 3. The author's purpose was to tell about how the Grimke sisters fought against slavery even though they grew up with slaves in their home. 4. The author's purpose was to describe the Underground Railroad and how people risked their lives to free slaves. 5. A plantation is a large property that is worked by live-in help. 6. An abolitionist was a person who fought to end slavery. 7. "The Grimke Sisters against Slavery": At first, they were taken care of by slaves. Then, they grew to hate slavery. Finally, they worked to end slavery. "Riding the Underground Railroad": At first, slaves wanted their freedom. Then, people joined together to make secret routes to get slaves to the North. Finally, many slaves escaped to freedom on the Underground Railroad. 8–9. Answers will vary but should clearly contrast or compare both passages.

Pages 67–68
1. It informs readers about how vegetables are grown on a farm. 2. 3, 2, 1, 4; 3. A; 4. It tells readers how a garden can be grown indoors. 5. B; 6. A; 7. Answers will vary but should include information from the passages such as (Farm Garden) First, till the soil. Next, plant the seeds. Then, water the crops. Last, pick the crops. (City Garden) First, cover the box bottom with plastic and pebbles, and then soil and fertilizer. Next, plant seed and plants in the soil. Then, water the plants with a watering can. Last, pick the vegetables.

8. Answers will vary but should include stated advantages and reasons including there is not much land in a city apartment, so garden boxes can be used to plant vegetables. Farms have access to more land and can get water from streams and rivers to water crops. Farms need workers to help plant and harvest what is grown. A garden box might provide enough vegetables for a family.

Pages 71–72
1. The author's purpose is to inform readers about what it is like for a young student to live and go to school in Mexico. 2. B; 3. Answers may include learning a new game, eating different foods, learning how to surf, learning to speak Spanish, and traveling to different cities. 4. The main idea is that living in a new place can be a great experience. 5. Answers may include walking to school, visiting France and Italy, learning to speak German, going on field trips, and attending Fasnacht. 6. B; 7. Answers will vary but may include (Mexico) traveling to different cities, learning Spanish, learning how to surf, eating new foods, playing loteria; (Switzerland) going on school field trips, visiting France and Italy, learning French and German, attending Fasnacht; (Both) traveling to a new country, learning a different language, eating unique foods, getting used to a new place to live; 8. Answers will vary but may include feeling scared and homesick. Both had to work to learn new languages. Each author experienced new things and enjoyed learning about a new culture.

Answer Key

Pages 75–76

1. The dog is being trained to be a guide dog. 2. D; 3. false; 4. Dogs can be helpful to people and warn of danger. 5. Maggie barked to warn her family of a bee's nest ahead on the path. 6. C; 7. Answers will vary but should include that Rocky was learning the patience to become a guide dog. Maggie was a brave dog who protected her family. Both dogs were intelligent and helped people. 8. Answers will vary but should include a comparison of both dogs' ability to learn and adjectives such as brave, smart, hardworking, and devoted.

Pages 79–80

1. A storm is coming and the sailors on the ship are braving the wind and waves. 2. It is poetry, shown because the passage has stanzas and lines that rhyme. 3. It is fiction. The person telling the story lives underwater. 4. Answers will vary but could include dark clouds coming, the ocean waves were rough, and it was windy. 5. Answers will vary but could include "like a ball bouncing," "seagulls bobbing up and down in the water," "waves are crashing," and "sand starts to blow in swirls." 6. C; 7. "A Life on the Ocean Wave" (See) rolling sea, sparkling foam; (Hear) winds and waters rave; (Feel) rolling sea; "On a Stormy Day" (See) storm clouds rolling in, seagulls bobbing on the water, sand swirling, a boat coming in; (Hear) wind picking up, waves crashing; (Feel) warm rays of the sun, spray of waves; 8. Answers will vary but could include how a storm might first seem threatening, but both characters enjoy the sights and sounds that come with a storm.

Pages 83–84

1. It is fiction (a poem) because the wind can think and talk. 2. The wind was trying to blow the moon out of the sky. The wind did not like to be watched by the moon. 3. No. The wind was blowing clouds around the moon to hide it. At the end of the passage, the moon is still in the sky. 4. It is fiction because people lived in the sky and tended the sun and moon. 5. D; 6. The children had to live in opposite parts of the sky so that they could not be near each other anymore. 7. "The Wind and the Moon" (Main Idea) The wind wants to blow away the moon. (Characters) the wind and the moon; (Problem) The wind tries but cannot blow the moon out of the sky. (Solution) The moon remains in the sky. "The Legend of the Moon" (Main Idea) tells how the moon came to be; (Characters) a boy, a girl, their father, the sun; (Problem) The children argue over who will tend to the sun. Because they are quarreling, the sun doesn't rise on time. (Solution) The children are separated in the sky with the boy tending the sun and the girl tending the moon. 8. Answers will vary but may include that in the poem the moon was something the wind could not move. The legend describes how and why the moon was created.

Pages 87–88

1. It is fiction. The passage is an imaginary story explaining how something happened. It has talking animals, which are not real. 2. Bear was angry because Chipmunk argued all night, and Bear did not get what he wanted. 3. B; 4. It is fiction (realistic). 5. B; 6. D; 7. Answers will vary but could include "How the Chipmunk Got Her Stripes" (Details) showed the other animals the sunrise, argued with Bear, angered Bear and was scratched; "The Missing Strawberry" (Details) liked ripe strawberries, was waiting for the right time to take the strawberry, hid from the boy; 8. Answers will vary but could include how each chipmunk was clever, quick, and kept trying to get what she wanted. Another story lesson could be that if you keep trying, anything is possible.

Pages 91–92

1. It is fiction because the shadow is treated like a character that can act on its own. 2. It is a poem because it has lines that rhyme, rhythm, and is written in stanzas. 3. It is fiction (realistic). 4. The passage is written as two letters. Each has a greeting, body, closing, and signature. 5. B; 6. C; 7. "My Shadow" (Main Idea) The shadow goes everywhere with the author. (Characters) the author, the shadow, (Problem/Solution) The shadow is too close to the author, but the shadow is missing if the author goes out very early in the morning. "The Dog Who Barks at Shadows" (Main Idea) Gabe needs help because his dog is barking at shadows all of the time. (Characters) Gabe, Toby, Dog's Best Friend, (Problem/Solution) Gabe's dog barks at every shadow he sees. The Dog's Best Friend suggests Gabe spend more time with Toby. 8. Answers will vary but should include a comparison of a shadow's role in each passage.